# INTERPRETED BY LOVE

# INTERPRETED BY LOVE

◆

An Anthology of Praise

COLLECTED BY
Elizabeth Basset

FOREWORD BY
Robert Runcie

DARTON · LONGMAN + TODD

First published in 1994 by
Darton, Longman and Todd Ltd
1 Spencer Court
140–142 Wandsworth High Street
London SW18 4JJ



ISBN 0–232–52072–0

A catalogue record for this book is available from the British Library

Cover: sculpture by Hilde Schürk-Frisch; design by Judy Linard

*All royalties earned by the sale*
*of this book will be donated to*
*World Community for Christian Meditation*
*23 Kensington Square*
*London W8 5HN*

Phototypeset in 10½/12½pt Bembo by Intype, London
Printed and bound in Great Britain at the University Press, Cambridge

O Sabbath rest by Galilee!
O calm of hills above,
Where Jesus knelt to share with thee
The silence of eternity,
Interpreted by love!

*The English Hymnal. 383*

*Dedicated to my grandsons*
*David, Michael and James*

# CONTENTS

FOREWORD
by Robert Runcie
*ix*

◆

INTRODUCTION
*xi*

◆

**I**
**I AM**
**Lord God of all Creation**
1

◆

**II**
**The World –**
**The Wonder of It**
19

◆

**III**
**The Journey**
**The Ongoing Revelation**
61

◆

**IV**
**Moments of Vision**
103

◆

**V**
**The Language of Silence**
123

◆

**VI**
**True Friendship**
147

◆

**VII**
**The Journey's End**
157

◆

ACKNOWLEDGEMENTS
175
INDEX OF AUTHORS
178

# FOREWORD

This is a lovely book. It perfectly completes Elizabeth Basset's quartet of anthologies. I am tempted to say 'You have kept the best wine . . .'.

The genius of Elizabeth Basset is to admit you to the company of her friends. What an assorted lot they are. Mystics rub shoulders with liberation theologians. She moves among them unobtrusively, with tact and good manners. She is not forever pointing the moral or adorning the tale. She has confidence in truth. Yet this is not just a commonplace book. It is skilfully woven, and we would do well to heed her gentle advice to explore the themes and not simply to pick at random.

In title and in style this collection is more contemplative than Elizabeth Basset's other anthologies. We sense someone who has not allowed our 'overcrowded' age to rob her of the power 'to approve the things that are excellent'.

'Be still', says the Psalmist 'and know that I am God'. There are stages on the way to that end: be still and know who you are; be still and find out who your friends are; be still and discover the world around you. Then, by the discipline of stillness thus learnt, you will be enabled to be still and know God himself, interpreted by love. This is the irresistible invitation which the author has so obviously heard and passes on so freshly to us.

# INTRODUCTION

I have often been asked what made me start collecting my anthologies.

For the first one, *Love Is My Meaning*, the idea came to me after a great sorrow in my family, the death of my youngest son at the age of eighteen. I started to write down quotations, prayers and songs, which I had found comforting in my despair.

Later I thought these might also be helpful to others going through their 'dark nights' and I had them printed privately and with great diffidence sent them to my friends.

The collection had to be reprinted several times and one of my friends showed it to Sir John Betjeman, who thought it should be published and sent it himself to the publisher. Since then it has been reprinted seven or eight times and is now in its second edition.

This has been a great joy to me. The letters from so many who have found the collection comforting have been beyond my wildest dreams.

I was asked to do a second anthology, which I called *Each In His Prison*. It was a collection of true stories of unbelievable courage, through the ages, many from the two World Wars, but also highlighting the fact that we are all prisoners of something in some way and that the only true freedom is given by God. 'Behold I come to set you free.'

Victor Frankel after his release wrote that his experiences in Auschwitz had proved to him that evil could never triumph over good. I remember at the launching of this book, replying to the kind things people had said and thanking them 'on behalf of those who had written the book with their lives'.

In my third anthology, *The Bridge Is Love*, I wanted to show that God speaks through the whole of His Creation – through

Nature, the Arts (through the Painter, the Musician, the Singer, the Sculptor, the Dancer), and through the joys and sufferings of life.

I think this latest collection combines all three of the motivations of the first three and I look upon *Interpreted By Love* as the last of the trilogy of the love of God for His Creation. It has three main themes: the *reality* of God; the fact that the purpose of our life on earth is an ongoing revelation and, finally, that there is an absolute necessity for us to be aware of the spiritual dimension of life. This awareness can, I believe, be realised supremely in the silence, the prayer of meditation.

The epitaph at the end of *Love Is My Meaning* is:

To Thee, O Lord
For Thee, O Lord
With Thee, O Lord
In Thee, O Lord,

and I think perhaps this is also part of the answer to those who ask me why I collected my anthologies: it shows my thankfulness that, through a long life, I have been given the grace to believe in God.

I have planned the sequence of the quotations deliberately. Whilst, like most anthologies, this is a book to be dipped into and not read from cover to cover, there is a certain thread which runs throughout, linking two or three quotations to each other, making the same point from different angles, in different forms, but revealing the same aspect of truth as I see it.

This arrangement reminds me of a phrase used by those 'shooting over dogs'. Two pointers work together, one scents the quarry and freezes stiff, still and pointing, while the other comes up and as he catches the same scent in his turn, he also freezes and this is called 'honouring the point'. I feel the writers I have quoted are honouring the point for one another, underlining its significance. I am most grateful to all those who have helped me in producing this collection – too many to mention by name. But there are a few people without whose constant encouragement it could never have been published: the late Bishop George Appleton; Clare Ziegler; Nigel Lynn; Fr Laurence Freeman OSB; Ian Warmington for his typing; Linda Redpath for the index; Lord Runcie for so kindly agreeing to write the foreword, and not forgetting those kind people who have given permission to use their work without charge.

◆ 1 ◆

# I AM
# Lord God of all Creation

◆ ***Prayer of St Augustine***

Lord let me offer you in sacrifice the service of my thoughts and my tongue, but first give me what I may offer to you.

◆ ***Lord God of All Creation*** by Siegfried Sassoon

AN OFFERING

Let there be life said God.
Let there be God say I.
Let life be God.

◆ *From* **Morning Has Broken** by Richard Harries

SOLZHENITSYN

It is above all his fierce integrity which comes across. His novels have the same quality of simple, abandoned truth-telling as those of Tolstoy; and he is totally uncompromising in his critique of both Marxism and Western Materialism. Then, like so many Russians and Dostoevsky in particular, he has this willingness to go to the heart of the matter. The key chapter in his novel *Cancer Ward* is called 'What men live by'.

He has made it quite clear what he himself lives by. He recalls a remark made to him as a child by older people trying to account for the disaster that had overtaken them: 'Men have forgotten God, that's why all this has happened'. All that has happened now includes the suffering of the Soviet Union since then, the First World War and the materialism of the Western World. 'If I were called upon to identify the principal trait of the twentieth century,' he has said, 'I would be unable to find anything more precise than to repeat once again – "Men have forgotten God".'

Solzhenitsyn's theme, if it came from anyone else, would be easy to shut one's ears to. He says many things we just don't want to hear. But coming from him, one is forced to listen to and take seriously what he says, to allow oneself and all one's assumptions to be questioned. Some people find him too sombre. Yet twice I saw the prophetic, bearded face irradiated with a warm lovely smile . . . Yet Solzhenitsyn makes it absolutely clear that his hope, this brightness he has within him, has a supernatural source; and though full of foreboding about the future of the world, he offers one way out. Instead of the ill-advised hopes of the last two centuries, which reduced us to insignificance and brought us to the brink of nuclear and non-nuclear death, he says, 'We can only reach with determination for the warm hand of God, which we have so rashly and self-confidently pushed away'.

Here is a prayer of Solzhenitsyn himself that I am very fond of because of its expression of total faith in God.

> How easy it is for me to live with you, Lord.
> How easy it is for me to believe in you.
> When my mind is distraught and my reason fails,
> When the cleverest people do not see further than this
> evening and do not know what must be done
> tomorrow,
> you grant me the clear confidence that you exist and
> that you will take care
> that all the ways of goodness are not stopped.
> And you will enable me to go on doing
> as much as needs to be done.
> And in so far as I do not manage it –
> that means that you have allotted the task to others.

◆ Archbishop Temple in his readings from St John's Gospel.

I AM

*When God told Moses to go and bring His people out of Egypt, Moses asked who he should say had sent him to them. God said to Moses, 'I AM WHO I AM . . . Say this to the people of Israel, I AM has sent me to you'.*

*This quotation from Exodus seems to me to be deeply significant for us today, when sadly so often God has seemed to be left out of the reckoning.*

*The theme of I AM is continued into the New Testament in the seven great I AM sayings of Christ in St John's Gospel. Archbishop Temple lists and describes them as follows:*

*(1) I am the Bread of Life. Christ nourishes us and gives us strength.*
*(2) I am the Light of the World. He gives us light to know the way we should follow in that strength.*
*(3) I am the Door of the Sheep. He is Himself the entrance into the fellowship of life.*
*(4) I am the Good Shepherd. He is the guardian of that fellowship who by His sacrifice wins for it new members.*
*(5) I am the Resurrection and the Life. He is Himself the life of that fellowship which lives in Him alone.*
*(6) I am the True Vine. He is even the fellowship itself for its members are incorporated into Him and it is His life that vitalises them.*
*(7) I am the Way, the Truth and the Life. Comprehensively He is Himself the Way to be followed in action, the Truth to be believed, the Life to be lived.*

*Before Abraham was I AM.*

◆ ***Alpha and Omega*** by Dorothea Eastwood

I am Alpha
I called you out of nothing into Form
I struck the dark to give you birth in Light
I am the source, incarnate in the Tree
The fruit my knowledge and the sap my love
I am Life
I am these green streams dancing in the blood
That prove your marriage with the summer grove
I am the Vine; the immortal Corn
And I the Breath
That interlinks you with the wide
Blue radiant acres of the air
  I am Fate:
  I am those gold-eyed planets that direct
  Your hesitant feet across the paths of earth
  I am Peace
  I am the look on any face

That finds even for a moment, love and truth
I am the Voice:
I call to break your sleep
I am Dawn:
I am the dream you seek for when you wake
In the tree, the stars, through Time and in
  the heart
Immanent spirit dwelling in your bone
I am Omega: I am. I AM.

◆ ***Prayer for Michaelmas*** by Viola Garvin, *taken from* **Uncommon Prayers** by Cecil Hunt

'*Nature is the art of God.*'
Sir Thomas Browne

Good St Michael, if we must
Leave our bodies here to dust
Grant our souls a heaven where we
Still your Michaelmas may see
Do not make me quire and sing
With radiant angels in a ring,
Nor idly tread a pearl-paved street
With my new unearthly feet;
Do not shut me in a heaven
Golden bright from morn to even,
Where no shadows and no showers
Dim the tedious, shining hours,
Grant that there be Autumn still,
Smoke-blue dusk, brown, crisp and chill,
And let the furrowed plough and bare
Curve strongly to the windswept air;
Make the leafy beechwoods burn
Russet, yellow, bronze by turn,
And set the hedgerow and the briar
Thick with berries red as fire.
Let me search and gather up
Acorns green with knobbed cup,
And prickly chestnuts, plumping down
To show a glossy kernel brown.

Splendid cities like me ill
And for song I have no skill;
Then let me in an Autumn wood
Sweep and pick up sticks for God.

◆ *Creation* by John Riches, aged thirteen, *taken from* **On Common Ground** by Jill Pirrie

Creation . . .
Nothingness, blackness, non-life.
A single spark, light as a
Moon starts a sun glowing,
Growing, winning its body by
A timeless dawn, the Alpha of
Omega, the grain of a mountain.
A world.
A spawn, an aspiring life roots
And begins. A movement.
The rustle, the learning spreads
As does the light.
It grows, multiplies;
Maybe a fish inheriting a past,
An eel or salmon but always
Life, Light.

◆ *From* **A Thousand Reasons for Living** by Dom Helder Camara

All absolutely all
by your grace
speaks to me of you.
When I write I ask in your name to be
The blank sheet of paper
Where you can write what you please.

When I skim through a book
I feel acutely anxious
That such a lot of words should not go fruitless
In that no one should write without some happy message to
the world.

Every step I take
reminds me of you
that wherever I am going
I am always on the march to eternity
all, all, all makes me think of you
What can I give to the Lord
For all he has given to me.

Of all our lessons master
one is so important
I forget about the rest
Teach me to reach for the infinite
the light which is on the horizon
helps heaven come down to earth
and earth reach up to heaven.

◆ ***Jeremiah 31:35–36***

Thus says the LORD,
who gives the sun for light by day
and the fixed order of the moon
and the stars for light by night,
who stirs up the sea so that its waves roar –
The LORD of hosts is his name.

◆ *From* **More Latin Lyrics** translated by Helen Waddell

BOETHIUS

There is no race of men
But rose from one same spring.
One Father of them all,
To all things giving.
He gave the sun his beams
The moon her crescent of light.
To earth he gave mankind,
Stars to the night.
Prisoner in body, soul
Besieged by heaven,
Mortality is sprung
From a noble stock.

Why bluster about race,
And brag of ancestry?
If you would look at that from whence you came,
God that begot you
Not one
Would prove a degenerate son
Or cling
To evil thing,
Lest he should lose his way
To his primeval spring.

◆ *From* **God As Spirit** by G.W.H. Lampe

Creation is not a past and finished act of God; it is going on now. Salvation is not a future act of God which has still to begin; it has been, and is, in progress from the beginning of the creation of men. God has always been incarnate in his human creatures, forming their spirits from within and revealing himself in and through them; for although revelation comes from beyond the narrow confines of the human spirit and is not originated by man himself, there is not, and never has been any revelation of God that has not been incarnated in, and mediated through, the thought and emotions of men and women.

◆ *From* **Christianity Rediscovered** by Vincent J. Donovan

We Christians profess to believe in a continuing creation. We believe that God is continuing to create and hold in existence the world and everything in it: the atom and the molecule, the mountain and the chair, the rocket hurtling through space, the television set, my finger and my mind: that if God ceased to exist, create, took away his creative presence, all these things and we ourselves, would cease to exist on the instant. This creative power is acting now and here.

The purpose of prayer is to open us up fully to that power.

◆ ***Jeremiah 31:33–34***

But this is the covenant which I will make with the house of Israel after those days, says the LORD: I will put my law within them, and I will write it upon their hearts; and I will be their God, and they shall be my people.

And no longer shall each man teach his neighbour and each his brother, saying, 'Know the LORD,' for they shall all know me, from the least of them to the greatest, says the LORD; for I will forgive their iniquity, and I will remember their sin no more.

◆ *From* **The Land Unknown** by Kathleen Raine

'Truly understood the entire world is one great symbol, imparting in a sacramental manner, by outward and visible signature, an inward and spiritual essence.'

The living world is our book of wisdom. It was Plato in ancient Greece who first described the realest of the real and the clearest of the clear as 'beauty' . . . To see spirituality as beauty and to see beauty in all things is the deep inspiration of Kathleen Raine's poetry.

◆ *From* **Weavers of Wisdom** by Anne Bancroft

KATHLEEN RAINE

I would like the young to feel that we are living spirits, we are living souls and children of the eternal spirit, which is the divine source of all things, the whole universe, as well as ourselves. I think from that all the rest follows. It means turning right round and looking the other way. Once you see that man bears the signature of God, then you *cannot* treat people in the way that people do treat each other.

When I say 'God', I explain it in this way. I see the divine Self – that which is – as a person. Not in the sense of a personified God or a deified man in the name of Jesus, but because the eternal and everlasting self has consciousness, has knowledge of all things, one speaks of a person rather than a life-force or anything of that kind; because mind, consciousness, sat-chit-ananda (being aware bliss) is a living being spirit, you see, and so I do believe in a divine being. One cannot speak of mind or consciousness without speaking of God as not *a* person, but as *The* person in the universe.

◆ *From* **The Hour of Glory** by George Appleton

We who profess to be Christ's disciples believe that God revealed himself in Christ in human form that all humans can understand.

We believe that God is the Creator and Father of us all. The redeemer of us all, that he wills to incarnate himself in each one of us.

We believe that in the cross God shows us his heart, the eternal heart that never ceases to love and forgive, whatever we do to him or his Christ.

If we really believe all that, we must surely believe that God is at work among all, starting where they are.

We must be interested in the spiritual nature and experience of people of other faiths.

We have no monopoly of God and Christ.

We must not dismiss others as heathen and pagan.

On the cross Christ died for all and everyone we meet is equally a brother or sister for whom Christ died, whatever may be his or her religious tradition or cultural milieu.

◆ *From* **The Gates of Heaven** by the Union of Progressive Synagogues, London

Religion is essentially the act of holding fast to God. And that does not mean holding fast to an image that one has made of God, nor even holding fast to the faith in God that one has conceived. It means holding fast to the existing God. The earth would not hold fast to its conception of the sun (if it had one), nor to its connection with it, but to the sun itself.

◆ *From* **The Alternative Service Book 1980**

Yours, God, is the greatness, the power, the glory, the splendour, and the majesty; for everything in heaven and earth is yours. All things come from you and of your own do we give you.

◆ *From* **The Festival of Faith and Environment**. Canterbury Cathedral

O Lord of every shining constellation
that which wheels in splendour through the midnight sky
grant us your Spirit's true illumination
to read the secrets of your work on high.

You, Lord have made the atom's hidden forces
your laws its mighty energies fulfil:
teach us to whom you give such rich resources,
in all we use to serve your holy will.

O life, awakening life in cell and tissue
from flower to bird, from beast to brain of man;
help us to trace, from birth to final issue,
the sure unfolding of your age-long plan.

You, Lord have stamped your image on your creatures,
and though they mar that image, love them still;
Lift up your eyes to Christ, that in his features
We may discern the beauty of your will.

Great Lord of nature, shaping and renewing,
You made us more than nature's sons to be;
you help us tread, with grace our souls enduring
the road to life and immortality.

◆ *From* **God Calling** – A Devotional Diary by Two Listeners, edited by A.J. Russell

I came to help a world. And according to the varying needs of each so does each man see Me.

It is not necessary that you see Me as others see Me – the world even the Church, My disciples, My followers, but it is necessary that You see Me, each of you as supplying all that you personally need.

The weak need Strength, My Strength. The strong need My Tenderness. The tempted and fallen need My Salvation. The righteous need My Pity for sinners. The lonely need a Friend. The fighters need a Leader.

No *man* could be all these to men – only a God could be. In each of these relations of mine to man you must see God. The God-friend, the God-leader, the God-Saviour.

◆ ***Hymn***

O LORD MY GOD. When I in awesome wonder
Consider all the works Thy hand has made

I see the stars, I hear the mighty thunder,
Thy power throughout the universe displayed.

Then sings my soul, my Saviour God to Thee
How great Thou art. How great Thou art.
Then sings my soul, my Saviour God to Thee
How great Thou art. How great Thou art.

When through the woods and the forest glades I wander
And hear the birds sing sweetly in the trees
When I look down from lofty mountains' grandeur,
And hear the brook and feel the gentle breeze.

*Chorus*

And when I think of God, His Son not sparing,
Sent Him to die – I scarce can take it in.
That on the Cross my burden gladly bearing
He bled and died to take away my sin.

*Chorus*

When Christ shall come with shout of acclamation
And take me home – what joy shall fill my heart;
Then shall I bow in humble adoration
And there proclaim, my God how great Thou art.

◆ *From* **The Song of the Bird** by Anthony de Mello

THE SONG OF THE BIRD

The disciples were full of questions about God
Said the Master, 'God is Unknown
The Unknowable. Every statement about
Him, every answer to your questions,
Is a distortion of the truth.'

The disciples were bewildered. 'Then
Why do you speak about Him at all?'

'Why does the bird sing?' said the Master,
'Not because he has a statement, but because he
has a song.'

The words of the Scholar are to be understood. The words of the Master are to be understood. They are to be listened to as one listens to the wind in the trees and the sound of the river and the song of the bird. They will awaken something within the heart that is beyond all knowledge.

◆ *From* **God As Spirit** by G.W.H. Lampe

Only God can create, man cannot make his own soul. But transcendent God creates man from within, as the immanent personal indwelling Spirit who inspires and guides and evokes that response of faith and love which is the human side of the relationship of sonship.

◆ ***Hymn*** by Timothy Rees (1874–1939) and Rowland Hugh Pritchard (1811–1887) sung at the King's School Canterbury Carol Service

God is Love: let heav'n adore him;
God is Love: let earth rejoice:
Let Creation sing before him;
And exalt him with one voice:
He who laid the earth's foundations
He who spread the heavens above.
He who breathes through all Creation
He is Love eternal Love.

God is Love and he enfoldeth
All the world in one embrace:
With unfailing grasp he holdeth
Every child of every race:
And while human hearts are breaking
Under sorrow's iron rod
Then they find that selfsame aching,
Deep within the heart of God.

God is Love: and though with blindness
Sin afflicts the soul of man,
God's eternal loving kindness
Holds and guides them even then.
Sin and death and hell shall never
O'er us final triumph gain:
God is Love, so Love forever
O'er the universe must reign.

◆ *From* **The Song of the Bird** by Anthony de Mello

DID YOU HEAR A BIRD SING?

Hindu India developed a magnificent image to describe God's relationship with Creation. God 'dances' Creation. He is the Dancer. Creation is his Dance. The dance is different from the dancer; yet it has no existence apart from him. You cannot take it home in a box, if it pleases you. The moment the dancer stops, the dance ceases to be.

In our quest for God, we think too much, reflect too much. Even when we look at this dance that we call creation, we are the whole time thinking, talking (to ourselves and others), reflecting, analysing, philosophising. Words. Noise.

Be silent and contemplate the Dance. Just look; a star, a flower, a fading leaf, a bird, a stone . . . any fragment of the Dance will do. Look, Listen, Smell, Touch, Taste. And, hopefully, it won't be long before you see Him – the Dancer Himself.

The disciple was always complaining to his Master, 'You are hiding the final secret of Zen from me' and he would not accept the Master's denials.

One day they were walking in the hills when they heard a bird sing. 'Did you hear a bird sing?' said the Master.

'Yes,' said the disciple.

'Well, now you know that I have hidden nothing from you.'

'Yes.'

If you really heard a bird sing, if you really saw a tree . . . you would know, beyond words and concepts.

What was that you said? You have heard dozens of birds sing and seen hundreds of trees? Ah, was it the tree you saw or the label? If you look at a tree and see a tree, you have really not seen the tree. When you look at the tree and see a miracle, then, at last, you have seen. Did your heart never fill with wordless wonder when you heard a bird in song?

◆ *From* **God of a Hundred Names**, collected by Barbara Greene

DHU'L-NUN, died 861. Sufi.

O God, I never hearken to the voices of the beasts or the rustle of the trees, the splashing of waters or the song of birds, the whistle of the wind or the rumble of thunder, but I sense in them a testimony to Thy Unity and a proof of Thy Incomparableness; that Thou art the All-prevailing, the All-knowing, the All-wise, the All-just, the All-true, and in Thee is neither overthrow, nor ignorance, nor folly, nor injustice, nor lying. O God, I acknowledge Thee in the proof of Thy handiwork and the evidence of Thy acts: grant me, O God, to seek Thy satisfaction with my satisfaction, and the Delight of a Father in His Child, remembering Thee in my love for Thee, with serene tranquillity and firm resolve.

◆ *From* **A Glimpse of Glory** by Gonville ffrench-Beytagh

LIGHT AS THE GLORY OF GOD

Of course the dazzling glory of God is there throughout the Bible. The story of the transfiguration shows his shining glory. Christ's face and his clothes were blazingly, blindingly, dazzlingly, bright and there was a bright cloud surrounding him. In Genesis, God says 'Let there be light' and the primordial light of God himself is there before the creation of the sun and moon and the stars. This kind of light is beyond our imagination.

Christ himself (in John 17:3) refers to 'the glory which I had with thee before the world was'. Though this glory is beyond our conceiving, it is not beyond our glimpsing. The light of the presence of God was there at the burning bush; the sight of the glory of God was like a devouring fire on the top of Mount Sinai; it accompanied the tabernacle in the wilderness, in the cloud by day, and the pillar of fire by night.

Lord, thy glory fills the heavens
Earth is with its fullness stored;
Unto thee be glory given
Holy, Holy, Holy Lord.

◆ *From* **Bread of the World** by John Hadley

The true moment of glory arises when the spark of God's glory hidden 'among the stuff' of his creation discovers an answering spark in the depths of our soul, and the two leap together in a single flame of adoration; in angelic terms when we hear the song of the angels and are able to respond, to join in their singing . . . 'Glory' is a characteristic of God, and also our response to him: we see his glory, we give him glory. But the true *experience* of glory comes in the fusion of the two, it is the moment of encounter and reconciliation between two apparently separate things, when the spark leaps from the one to the other and back again, and the differences melt away and the underlying unity of all things is revealed. So we experience glory not only at 'religious' moments but at any 'moment of truth': when we perceive a pattern in things for the first time, when everything suddenly 'makes sense', when a piece of music; or a painting; or a place speaks directly to our soul, when we fall in love. All such moments of 'cosmic disclosure', as Bishop Ian Ramsay put it, are a potential source of conversion, of a new life and inspiration, whether we choose to frame them in theological language or not; whether our response is 'Glory be', or something less pious.

. . . To be the vehicle of the glory of God is essential to being the son of God, to being truly human. So it was for Jesus, and so it is to be for us.

◆ ***Gerard Hughes***

'Each one of us has this one thing to do. To let God's glory through.'

◆ *From* **Bread of the World** by John Hadley

PENITENCE

Of course the very suggestion of penitence helps guard us against the smugness of the Pharisee, so certain that he is justified before God; but isn't there a subtler danger, that we become a sort of hybrid? Praying Lord, have mercy on me a sinner, so that when you have had mercy, I may become like the Pharisee, whereas our vocation is always to stay with Christ among the sinners.

The danger is of too easy forgiveness, a too light healing of the wound. For one thing, who am I to assess my own sins, to know which are the grave ones and which the petty?

Once in a contrite passion
I cried out in my grief.
And said, 'O Lord have mercy
Of sinners I'm the chief'.
Then came a kindly angel,
And standing just behind,
Said, 'Vanity, my little man:
You're nothing of the kind'.

For me to judge my own sins would be like a physician healing himself or a poet explaining his own poetry; others usually see so much better from a distance. The things that worry me most may actually be unimportant; while my gravest sins may in fact be things that hardly occur to me, even things I'm not aware of.

◆ 2 ◆

# The World – The Wonder of It

## INTRODUCTION TO THE WORLD

*Bishop John Taylor once wrote, 'It is not more wonders that we need but more WONDER'. If we have eyes to see we can glimpse the Creator in all His Creation. In the words of George Tardios:*

*The World is troubled*
*With the lack of looking.*

*We can see Him in the trees, the flowers, the rivers, the mountains, the birds and the beasts and the butterflies. The Mystery of Life. The rivers speak to us in their own way, so many different ways, so do the mountains and the trees.*

*Sadly we seem to have lost so much of our communication with Nature, a communion which was so obviously enjoyed by the more primitive peoples of the world, but is, I think, still experienced by those who live close to Nature.*

*I think of the mountaineer risking his life to conquer the heights; the sailor and all who find their living on the sea; perhaps most of all the gallant lifeboatmen risking their lives to save life.*

*I think of the farmer watching the furrow being ploughed on his land and all who have a part to play in creation. Of the newborn baby, the foal, the calf, or the puppy. All these must be aware of the Creator in the created. They are the people who in Gerard Manley Hopkins' words, 'Perceive the AH in things'. E.B.*

◆ ***Wonder*** by Mary Gilmore

Give life its full domain and feed the soul
With wonder, find within the clod a world
Or gazing on the rounded dewdrop purled
Upon a leaf, mark how its tiny bowl
Includes the sun, that sun in whose control
The planets run their courses, and the furled

Comet, onward driven, resists what hurled
It downward, outward to its nether goal.

◆ *From* **Gardens of the Mind** by Joan Law-Smith

O, as a child, how often have I stood
And watched a turning furrow, beauty spelled
That rhythm, that curve of moving earth that felled
In endless seam upon the narrowing rood,
Not e'en the sea itself has me so held
So to my heart brought full beatitude.

◆ *From* **Who Is This?** by Eric James. Address in Holy Week, April 1990

BY PROFESSOR JOHN MACQUARRIE ON MYSTERY AND TRUTH

There is today a revival of interest and the sense of wonder in our secular society especially among the young people. This may mark the beginning of a revulsion against the long-established hostility to mystery in Western philosophy.

Now it is true that the most natural (if not the only) way into mystery is through the exploration of man himself. The Christian faith is singularly well situated to give a lead in the quest for mystery. By its doctrine of the Incarnation Christianity holds that it is precisely in a human person, Jesus Christ, that the final mystery of being has been opened up. According to Paul Christ is the revelation of the mystery which was kept secret for long ages (Romans 16:25–26).

This is commonly taken to mean that Christ has revealed and opened up the mystery of God. But would it not be correct to say that he has done this by opening up the mystery of man? Is there not a deep affinity between the mystery of God and the mystery of humanity? By becoming man in the fullest sense, that is to say in a measure of fullness that transcends all our ordinary levels of manhood, Christ manifests God in the flesh.

He pushes back the horizons of the human mystery so that they open to the divine mystery but he does so without ceasing to be man.

It is in response to that divine mystery that we are invited to

'Prise open the Alabaster Box of our heart, our feelings, our body and mind, our intellect and our soul. 'Who is this?' I want to answer: 'It is the one who enables us who are human to prise open the mysterious Alabaster Box that is uniquely ours. But I want you to be able to make your own answer, your own response, with the mysterious Alabaster Box that is yours'.

◆ *From* **Bread of the World** by John Hadley

GLORIA

THE WONDER OF THE WORLD

If the blaze (of glory) is to become true fire, it needs an answering flare from the heart of the beholder. We rarely see angels: not because they aren't there, but because we are not attuned to them, we are too preoccupied with a more mundane wavelength. I once met a woman in a London park who, after going on at some length about the beauty of what lay around, ended her remarks with the memorable sentence: 'It is important to be thrilled by all this'. We need to cultivate the seed of glory sown at our birth – a theme dear to the Romantic poets like Wordsworth and Lermontov:

An angel flew through the midnight sky
And a gentle song he sang;
And the moon and the stars and the company of clouds
Listened to the holy song.
He sang of the bliss of sinless souls
Under the tents of heavenly gardens;
Of God in his greatness he sang,
And his praise was unfeigned.
In his arms he carried a young soul,
For the world of grief and tears
And within the young soul the sound of his song
Remained without words, but alive.
And it languished long in the world,
Full of wonderful longing,
And the sounds of heaven could not be erased
Within it by the dull songs of earth.

◆ *From* **Being in Love** by William Johnston

To be open to this mysterious and obscure sense of presence. God is there in the mountains and the oceans, in the flowers and the birds, in the trees and the fields. Walk through the green fields or the brown bog; or walk beside the ocean, listening to every sound, aware of the beauty, and above all conscious of the enveloping presence that hovers over everything. This can be exhilarating prayer. For God is wonderfully present in all things, working in all things, giving himself to us in all things . . . We cannot see him or touch him, but we can sometimes sense his presence, his healing presence. When your heart or mind be troubled, walk and look at nature. Feel the air and the rain washing your body and cleansing your spirit. Eat and drink copiously from the emerging, liberating, healing, life-giving table of life.

Finally, while I have urged you to pray in the midst of nature with flowers of the field and birds of the air, I also urge you to pray in the mighty city. In the whirl and bustle of Fifth Avenue or Piccadilly you can pause for a moment to feel the presence of a reality that transcends everything: you can be aware of a world of enlightenment which transcends the phenomenal world that meets your eye. Teilhard de Chardin was aware of the presence of an all-loving God in the factories and shipyards and airports. God is everywhere and in everything. As you search for him never forget that he is also searching for you.

◆ *From* **The Festival of Faith and Environment**. Canterbury Cathedral September 15th, 1989

Lord of beauty, thine the splendour
shown in earth and sky and sea,
burning sun and moonlight tender,
hill and river, flower and tree:
lest we fail our praise to render
teach our eyes that we may see.

Lord of wisdom, whom obeying
mighty waters ebb and flow,
While unhasting, undelaying,
planets on their courses go

in thy laws thyself displaying,
teach our minds thyself to know.

Lord of life, alone sustaining
all below and all above,
Lord of love, by whose ordaining
sun and stars sublimely move,
In our earthly spirits reigning,
lift our hearts that we may love.

Lord of beauty, bid us own thee,
Lord of truth, our footsteps guide,
till as love our hearts enthrone thee:
and with vision purified,
Lord of all, when all have known thee,
thou in all art glorified.

◆ *From* **The Earth in Balance** by HRH The Prince of Wales. May 23rd 1990 BBC TV

The Greeks and Romans lived near Nature and saw the earth as a living organism; the historian Xenophon spoke of the earth as a divine being who rewarded those who protected her and punished those who didn't.

. . . There's nothing new about ecological destruction; what is new is the awesome power that modern science and technology has put into man's hands.

We really can move mountains and cause whole forests to come tumbling down, erase whole forests in the twinkling of an eye, but science and technology can't put them back as they were.

◆ *From* **Language of the Trees**. The Seneca Indian Historical Society, New York

TWYLAH NITSCH

The real Seneca feeling was to do with the mysteries of Mother Earth. To learn about her secrets was to learn about oneself . . .

Self-knowledge was the key
Self-understanding was the desire

Self-discipline was the way
Self-realization was the goal.

Entering into the silence.

Living in harmony with the peace and quietude of Nature, taught the Seneca self-discipline. They moved slowly, spoke softly, and developed a natural quiescence. This silence had to be learnt and signified perfect harmony in spirit, mind and body. To master this characteristic meant functioning harmoniously within one's immediate environment.

In addition to Nature's silence Mother Earth offered many symbolic examples, some of which were shapes . . . for example, the circle – the sun, the moon, the water and the earth.

Life, to the early Seneca, had great significance. It was the manifestation of the Life-Force of the Great Mystery or the Great Spirit. It was expressed by one's health, in spirit, mind and body. All American Indians believed that the Spiritual Essence was perfect, a state of perfection, totally balanced in Nature on every dimension of existence. The purpose in life was to develop one's natural potentials and share these gifts with others.

◆ *From* **A Quickening Joy** by Mary Spain

As though a deaf musician, I am part
Of some great orchestra I cannot hear.
The only notes that fall upon my ear
Are those which rise unbidden from the heart
And offer teasing glimpses of the art
Of harmony. Yet have I heard, in clear
Still moments of perception, what appear
As distant drum-beats; pulses that impart
A rhythm to the cosmic melody.
Then, with a quick'ning joy, I see that I
Am moving to creation's symphony.
As birds that wheel and dart across the sky
To secret music, so it seems that we
Can sometimes see the patterns as we fly.

◆ *From* **In Search of a Way** by Gerard Hughes

Reflect how God dwells in creatures, in the elements giving them existence, in the plants giving them life, in the animals conferring on them sensations: so he dwells in me and gives me being, life, sensation, intelligence, and makes a temple of me since I am created in the likeness and image of the divine majesty.

Thoughts from this contemplation passed through my mind as I looked at the sea and the sky, and the plants and the animals.

The truth was overwhelming, like waves breaking over me, sweeping me out of myself and leaving me speechless.

Prayer is so different from thinking. Thinking is like preparing the route before climbing a mountain, praying is the climb itself, a totally different experience.

◆ *From* **The Times**, Saturday September 2nd 1989, by Gillian Crow, a member of the Russian Orthodox Church

'SORTING THE BURIED TREASURE FROM THE RECYCLED RUBBISH'

God created the world for humans so that through it they should live in communion with Him. Creation was an act of love, and the response should be one of love. Man's role, therefore, is to love the world, to see it as transparent to God, to care for it with tenderness, to offer it back to Him in love.

The two statements – of the world belonging to man and man belonging to the world – are not opposed. Man is a part of the world made from its material; he belongs to it in the most basic sense as well as in a 'religious' sense, being part of God's creative act. And he is set at its centre to unite it to Him in an act of blessing, thanksgiving and adoration. That is a sacramental function. Mankind – that is, every human being, man, woman and child – is called to be not only king of Creation but also its priest. A priest serves, a priest offers, a priest consecrates. It is a process of giving, not asking.

. . . There is a vast store of such truth, the precious pearl waiting to be unearthed.

◆ *From* **The Everlasting Mercy** by John Masefield

O Christ who holds the open gate
  O Christ who drives the furrow straight
O Christ the plough, O Christ the laughter
  Of holy whitebirds flying after
Lo all my heart's field red and torn.

And thou wilt bring the young green corn
  The young green corn divinely springing
The young green corn for ever singing
  And when the field is fresh and fair
The blessed feet will glitter there.

And we will walk the weeded field
  And tell the golden harvest's yield
The corn that makes the holy bread
  By which the soul of man is fed
The holy bread the food unpriced
  Thy everlasting mercy, Christ.

◆ ***The Flower*** by R.S. Thomas

I asked for riches
You gave me the earth, the sea,
  the immensity
Of the broad sky. I looked at them
And learned I must withdraw to possess them.
I gave my eyes and my ears, and dwelt
  in a soundless darkness
  in the shadow of your regard.
The soul grew in me filling me
  with its fragrance.
Men came to me from the four winds to hear me
  speak of the unseen flower by which

I sat, whose roots were not
in the soil, nor its petals the colour
of the wide sea, that was its own species with
its own sky over it, shot
with the rainbow of your coming and going.

◆ *From* **The Garden of the Beloved** by Robert Way

Said the disciple to the Lover, 'Sir, before I left the world I heard certain men who were held in high esteem and thought to know the will of the Beloved say that those who loved the beautiful did not love the Beloved but loved idols. Yet in the garden of the Beloved we are ever striving to create beauty for the pleasure of the Beloved. Were they then speaking the truth?'

The Lover answered, 'Those who said this had never glimpsed the form of the Beloved nor ever truly sought Him, for all beauty is but the reflection of the goodness of the Beloved, so it is that those who love beauty and goodness and recognise dimly in them the form of the Beloved, and though often in ignorance, those who are seeking the Beautiful and the Good are seeking after the Beloved.'

◆ *From* **Touching Beauty's Hand** by Gwendy Caroe

Should I fail to see
Grace in flower and tree
I had not seen
My Lord's grace
Had I been in Galilee.

Should I fail to hear
The song of earth ring clear,
How may the Spirit's voice
With small noise
Catch my ear?

But if I listening stand
Touching Beauty's hand
And watching wait,

Might I perceive
Or soon or late
My Lord's command?

◆ *From* **Hymn to Intellectual Beauty** by Percy Bysshe Shelley

The awful shadow of an unseen power
Floats though unseen among us – visiting
This various world with as inconstant wing
As summer winds that creep from flower to flower –
Like moonbeams that behind some piny mountain shower
It visits with inconstant grace
Each human heart and countenance
Like hues and harmonies of evening –
Like clouds in starlight widely spread –
Like memory of music fled –
Like aught that for its grace may be
Dear, and yet dearer for its mystery.

◆ *From* **Collected Poems** by Walter De La Mare

THE SCRIBE

What lovely things
Thy hand hath made
The smooth plumed bird
In its emerald shade
The seed of the grass
The speck of stone
Which the wayfaring ant
Stirs and hastes on.

Though I should sit
By some tarn on thy hills
Using its ink
As the spirit wills
To write of earth's wonders
Its live, willed things

Flit would the ages
On soundless wings
Ere unto Z

My pen drew nigh;
Leviathan told,
And the honey-fly
And still would remain
My wit to try –
My worn reed broken,
The dark tarn dry
All words forgotten –
Thou Lord and I.

◆ ***For Birds*** by an Arab Chieftain, *from* **God of a Hundred Names**

I listen with reverence to the birdsong ascending
At dawn from the oasis, for it seems to me
There is no better evidence for the existence of God
Than in the bird that sings, though it knows not why
From a spring of untrammelled joy that wells up in its heart
Therefore I pray that no sky-hurled hawk may come
Plummeting down,
To silence the singer, and disrupt the Song
That rhapsodic, assured transcending song
Which foretells and proclaims when the Plan is worked out,
Life's destiny: the joyous, benign Intention of God.

◆ ***Hymn*** by Eleanor Farjeon (1881–1965)

Morning has broken
Like the first morning,
Blackbird has spoken
Like the first bird.
Praise for the singing!
Praise for the morning!
Praise for them, springing
Fresh from the Word!

Sweet the rain's new fall
Sunlit from heaven,
Like the first dewfall
On the first grass.
Praise for the sweetness
Of the wet garden,
Sprung in completeness
Where his feet pass.

Mine is the sunlight!
Mine is the morning
Born of the one light
Eden saw play!
Praise with elation,
Praise every morning,
God's re-creation
Of the new day!

◆ *From* **More Latin Lyrics** translated by Helen Waddell

BOETHIUS

This bird was happy once in the high trees.
You cage it in your cellar, bring it seed,
Honey to sip, all that its heart can need
Or human love can think of till it sees,
Leaping too high within its narrow room,
The old familiar shadows of the leaves,
And spurns the seed with tiny desperate claws
Naught but the woods despairing pleads
The woods, the woods again, it grieves, it grieves.

◆ ***Swans at Night*** by Mary Gilmore, *taken from* **Gardens of the Mind** by Joan Law-Smith

Within the night, above the dark
I heard a host upon the air
Upon the void they made no mark
For all that they went sailing there

And from that host there came a cry
A note of calling strange and high;
I heard it blown against the sky
Till naught there seemed but it and I.

A long and lonely wraith of sound
It floated out in distance wide
As though it knew another bound,
A space wherein it never died.

I heard the swans, I heard the swans
I heard the swans that speed by night;
That ever, where the starlight wanes,
Fly on unseen within the height.

I never knew how wide the dark
I never knew the depth of space
I never knew how frail a bark
How small is man within his place.

Not till I heard the swans go by,
Not till I marked their haunting cry
Not till, within the vague on high,
I watched them pass across the sky.

O trackless birds far journeying,
What guide have you, or swift or slow,
To give you trust in strength of wing
That must upbear you as you go?

What mark is set before your way?
What urging burns within the heart,
What bids you at the close of day
Uplift the wing of your depart?

What visions drawn from inner sight
Declare to you the way to go:
What power upholds you in your flight
To that unknown you cannot know?

I heard against the phantom sky
The swans their hollow music cry.
I felt the loneliness on high,
The dark where they went sailing by.

They say the swans sing but for death,
They say he wants in height to die;
Has he no more than that sharp breath
That whistles outward on his cry?

Is he but offspring of a vast
Where no hand shaped but gusty chance?
That draws no future from the past?
That moves unconscious of advance?

Nay, though we were but shaken dust,
Nay, though in darkness still we went,
We still must measure by our trust
The power that lifting o'er us bent;

And he who held within his hand
The trackless bird, by night and day,
Guided him out by sea and land,
His hand will never cast away.

I never knew how vast the sky,
I never knew how small was I,
Until I heard, remote and high,
The distant swans' far floated cry.

## THE NIGHT THE MOON THE STARS

◆ *From* **The Friend** 25.12.81. Ralph Waldo Emerson

Teach me your mood O patient stars.
Who climb each night the ancient sky.

Leaving on space no shade, no scars.
No trace of age, no fear to die.

◆ *From* **Poems** by Dorothea Eastwood

NIGHT

In Heaven, they say there is an end of Night:
That through the eternal radiance
Of the endless day, light glides to light.
In never ending streams of shining rays,
And we are told how in that exquisite, vibrant air
Not the least stain of shadow may impair
Its bright translucency.

So I suppose the coralled elms of March
Will not recall themselves upon the evening grass,
Nor cloudy shapes pursue
Their white, uplifted counterparts on windy days,
And patch the steady hills with dying blue.
So too the gay parade
Of chequered pattern in the woods will go,
We shall not see the Hazel nor the Oak
Travel in the leafy seas with nets of shade;
Nor yet the daffodil shadow her trumpet
With her creamy blades,
As down she bends before the long caresses of
the wind.

And yet perhaps, for less of this small dark
Such loveliness of light will make amends,
Though I must doubt.
But Oh dear God surely the moon will rise
For us again? Surely her great bronze globe
Will roll triumphant through the admiring skies?
And in the dawns of spring
May we not still behold her fragile horn
That clasps within its delicate white rim
The shining circlet of her perfect self?
Grant too we yet may see

The fields and hills curve sculptured by her beams,
While lakes lie watching her with silver eyes
And all the trees stand motionless in dreams.

And your night wandering beasts?
Otter and fox and deer
They cannot steal on small soft-footed ways
By glare of light;
Nor furry cubs venture to tumbling play
Except when flowers and leaves
Stand still at dusk and dawn.
Owls too, prick-eared, round-faced
Like gold-eyed cats
Will they crouch blinking through the eternal Day?
Or will they be flown and gone?
And never haunt the tall celestial woods
To creep the feathers of the moaning doves
With hollow shouts?
And fields will miss them if they are not there
To glide at dusk above the ploughlands' floating
    white mist breath,
In silent glimmering curve.

Oh truth is no more Beauty if indeed 'tis true
That God forbids his dark to Paradise;
But I would sooner face the withering spark
Than be denied the night
And if at times I could not lie
Within her quiet impartial arms,
Not all the bliss of Heaven
Nor all the ecstasy and shining charms,
Could recompense my soul for loss of her.

◆ *From* **Selected Poems** 1957–81 by Ted Hughes

THE HARVEST MOON

The flame-red moon, the harvest moon,
Rolls along the hills, gently bouncing,
A vast balloon,

Till it takes off, and sinks upward
To lie in the bottom of the sky, like a gold
doubloon.

The harvest moon has come,
Booming softly through heaven, like a bassoon,
And earth replies all night, like a deep drum

So people can't sleep,
So they go out where oaks and elms keep
A kneeling vigil, in a religious hush,
The harvest moon has come.

And all the moonlit cows and all the sheep
Stare up at her, petrified, while she swells
Filling heaven, as if red hot, and sailing
Closer and closer like the end of the world.

Till the gold fields of stiff wheat
Cry 'We are ripe, reap us' and the rivers
Sweat from the melting hills.

◆ *From* **The Merchant of Venice** by William Shakespeare

How sweet the moonlight sleeps upon this bank!
Here will we sit, and let the sounds of music
Creep in our ears: soft stillness and the night
Become the touches of sweet harmony.
Sit, Jessica: look, how the floor of heaven
Is thick inlaid with patines of bright gold:
There's not the smallest orb which thou behold'st
But in his motion like an angel sings,
Still quiring to the young-eyed cherubim;
Such harmony is in immortal souls;
But, whilst this muddy vesture of decay
Doth grossly close it in, we cannot hear it.

◆ ***Christmas Carol*** by E.H. Sears

It came upon the midnight clear,
That glorious song of old,
From angels bending near the earth
To touch their harps of gold:
'Peace on the earth, goodwill to men,
From heaven's all-gracious King!'
The world in solemn stillness lay
To hear the angels sing.

Still through the cloven skies they come,
With peaceful wings unfurled;
And still their heavenly music floats
O'er all the weary world;
Above its sad and lowly plains
They bend on hovering wing;
And ever o'er its Babel sounds
The blessed angels sing.

Yet with the woes of sin and strife
The world has suffered long;
Beneath the angel-strain have rolled
Two thousand years of wrong;
And man, at war with man, hears not
The love-song which they bring:
O hush the noise, ye men of strife,
And hear the angels sing.

And ye, beneath life's crushing load,
Whose forms are bending low,
Who toil along the climbing way
With painful steps and slow,
Look now! for glad and golden hours
Come swiftly on the wing;
O rest beside the weary road,
And hear the angels sing.

For lo! the days are hastening on,
By prophet-bards foretold,
When, with the ever-circling years,
Comes round the age of gold;
When peace shall over all the earth
Its ancient splendours fling,
And the whole world give back the song
Which now the angels sing.

◆ *From* **Selected Poems 1957–1981** by Ted Hughes

SONG

O lady, when the tipped cup of the moon blessed you
You became soft fire with a cloud's grace.
The difficult stars swam for eyes in your face,
You stood and your shadow was my place
You turned, your shadow turned to ice
O my lady.

O lady, when the sea caressed you
You were a marble of foam, but dumb,
When will the stone open the tomb?
When will the waves give over their foam?
You will not die, nor come home,
O my lady.

O lady, when the wind kissed you
You made him music for you were a shaped shell
I follow the waters and the wind still
Since my heart heard it and all to pieces fell
Which your lovers stole, meaning ill,
O my lady.

O lady, consider when I shall have lost you
The moon's full hands, scattering waste,
The sea's hands, dark from the world's breast,
The world's decay where the wind's hands have
passed
And my head, worn out with love, at rest.

In my hands, and my hands full of dust
O my lady.

◆ ***Clouds and the Moon*** by Anna Margaret Mitchell, aged six

The moon was racing towards me
Through an archway of clouds
Like a proud horse
Riding the silent clouds
Dark trees like servants
Bowling before it.

A light shining in the sky
With clouds dancing round it
The savage moon
Bites the clouds
Bits are ripped off and left.

Long thin strands of clouds
Holding the moon up
To be examined
Like forceps holding a pearl.

Sometimes the sky
Is dull and dark
A curtain of clouds
Is drawn across the moon
And it is time to sleep.

◆ ***Clouds*** by Dorothea Eastwood

See how these clouds, with tips of ostrich plume
Lean down to fan the sun before he goes.
And how he rests delighted on the hill
To watch the feathers quiver, gold and rose.

And now his time has come and he must plunge
To empty-skied Antipodes while soon

The clouds will change their fans to pearl and
white
With silver fringes to enchant the moon.

## MOUNTAINS

◆ *From* **The Book of Common Prayer**, Psalm 121:1–2

A SONG OF ASCENTS

I will lift up mine eyes unto the hills from whence cometh my help. My help cometh from the LORD who has made heaven and earth.

## MOUNTAINS AND HILLS

*There is something about mountains and hills which induces that soaring feeling, even to those of us who have not experienced the thrills and dangers of mountain climbing.*

*I think of my first sight of the magnificent, snow-covered Atlas range of giants, seen from Marrakesh. Of walking in the mountains from Saas Fee. The flowers, drifts of Gentians, Pulsatilla Anemones, Soldanellas and, in the valleys, Narcissi and Carnations. The streams and peaks.*

*In the high hills you come upon a flower which perhaps no one else will ever see, growing in its perfection just for the joy of 'being' and responding to its Creator.*

*I think of Deeside in the Spring. The birch trees bursting into the freshest, greenest of leaf, surrounded by the eternal silent hills which have been there for ever and, please God, will never change, though we have done our best – or should I say our worst – to mar their beauty by planting trees up to and over their skylines.*

*I think of an early morning sortie to watch the Capercailzie and the Blackcock lekking, displaying their beauty and their dominance. And in the Autumn hearing the Red Deer roaring in the mists, that eerie, mysterious sound echoing from hill to hill.*

*I remember a pair of Golden Eagles at Strathavon hunting down a valley. We were above them and could see the gold of their feathers. So often they can only be seen silhouetted against sky and the golden gleam has to be taken on trust.*

*How inadequate are my descriptions, but in the following quotations I feel the writers have been able to convey some of the grandeur, the deepfelt thankfulness that these things ARE.*

◆ *From* **Walk to Jerusalem** by Gerard Hughes

Born in Scotland, I am a prejudiced observer of the scenery.

There is a beguiling quality in the Scottish hills. When walking there on my own I have never felt lonely or even alone, for they seem friendly, yet speak of mystery. This experience helped me to understand what the early Fathers of the Church meant when they wrote of creation itself as being a sacrament of God, sign and effective sign of his presence.

Every bush is burning, if only we have eyes to see.

COME YE APART

Come ye apart into the mountains and rest awhile and breathe in the very breath of God to give thee life again.

*This was written by someone who had experienced the marvellous silence to be found only in the mountains – the silence of eternity.*

*(Source unknown)*

God of the hills, grant me strength to go back to the cities
without faltering.
Strength to go back to my daily tasks without tiring with
enthusiasm.
Strength to help my neighbour who has no hills to
remember.
God of the seas, grant me thy peacefulness, peace
to bring to the world of hurry and confusion.

Grant me self-control for the unexpected emergency,
patience
for wearisome tasks and contentment in small things.
God of the stars, may I take back the gift of
friendship, of love for all.
God of the earth, may I live out the truth that
Thou hast taught us.

◆ *From* **Uncommon Prayers**, collected by Cecil Hunt

*In quietness and confidence shall be your strength* (Isaiah 30:15)

O God of mountains, stars and boundless spaces.
O God of freedom: and of joyous hearts.
When Thy Face looketh forth from all men's faces:
Brood Thou around me, and the noise is o'er;
Thy universe my closet with shut door.

(*George Macdonald*)

'Tis good Lord to be here!
But we may not remain;
And since thou bidst us leave the mount
Come with us to the plain.

(*J. Armitage Robinson*)

◆ *From* **Speak to the Hills** by Geoffrey Winthorpe Young

HOLDING THE HEIGHTS

I have not lost the magic of long days:
I live them, dream them still
Still am I master of the starry ways
  and freeman of the hill.
Shattered my glass ere half the strands had run.
I hold the heights, I hold the heights I won.

Mine still the hope that hailed me from each height
  mine the unresting flame:
With dreams I charmed each doing to delight,
I dream my rest the same.
Severed my skein ere half the strands were spun –
I hold the dreams, I hold the dreams I won.

What if I love no more those kingly days?
  there night sleeps rock me still;

I dream my feet upon the starry ways
My heart rests in the hill.

I may not grudge the little left undone,
I hold the heights, I keep the dreams I won.

## RIVERS

*I love the idea that our journey through life can be likened to the pilgrimage of a river traced from its source to its eventual absorption by the ocean.*

*The small bubbling spring, the milky white glacier water, the Scottish beer-brown burn with the floating froth waiting to be 'blown', the crystal clear chalk stream, harbouring the brown trout tempting the fishermen to pit their patience and their skill to outwit them, the silent, slow-moving streams through the water meadows. In imagination the huge rivers loaded with tree trunks from the desecrated rain forests. The roaring torrents which can burst their banks causing such dire destruction. The Torridge in winter, huge plates of floating ice, a miniature Volga.*

*All making their way to the sea.*

*And what of the sea, the ocean that receives them? The flying fish, the dolphins, the gulls which miraculously keep pace with the ship, effortlessly, seemingly without moving their wings.*

*I think of the Pentland Firth, where the North Sea meets the Atlantic and at high tide throws up great jets of spray, known as the Merry Men of Mey.*

*The Atlantic rollers, the small rippling wavelets on the beaches. The rock pools and the sea anemones. The miraculous little Groatie Buckies, better known as cowrie shells.*

*The storms at sea, the courage of the lifeboatmen and their wives and children waiting and praying for their safe return. E.B.*

◆ *Extract from* **The Legend of St Dderfel** by Edward Knatchbull-Hugesen (1825–1895)

It always seems as if the Spirit of the River was speaking to me and telling me how, in its rapid, continuous course it is setting an example to man how he can most wisely and happily regulate his life. The water is so wise, when it comes to little banks and uneven places in its bed, it gently flows over them without making any bother about it, and this says the river, is just the way in which men should treat the little unpleasantnesses and smaller misfortunes of life instead of allowing such things to distract and worry them, and perhaps even to alter their whole course of existence. Then when huge boulders of rock stand out into the stream, the river glides quietly round them, accepting them as necessary evils which must be endured, since they cannot be cured, which is the way in which men should treat the greater difficulties and hardships of their lives, instead of fuming and fretting, or sitting down in despair. These are things that rivers never do, says the Spirit, and moreover as they constantly move forward, they explore with their water every hole and corner within their reach, neglecting nothing, giving a kindly wash to everything that comes in their way, and holding a pleasant conversation with all objects, living or inanimate, with which they come in contact. So a wise man, who desires to make his life useful and pleasant to himself and others will always seek for information as he goes along through the world, will have a cheery word for his fellow travellers and be ready to do a kind and friendly action to any that require it. And if he does so, just as the river grows broader and wider as it nears the ocean in which it finally loses itself and merges its waters in the infinite space of the sea, so the man's life will become grander and more noble as it approaches its close, and he will have gained the affection and respect of all whose respect and affection are worth gaining before the stream of his life, too, flows out upon the ocean of eternity.

◆ *From* **The Holy Bible**, Revelation 22:1–2

THE RIVER

Then he showed me the river of the water of life, bright as crystal, flowing from the throne of God and of the Lamb through the middle of the street of the city; also, on either side of the river, the tree of life with its twelve kinds of fruit, yielding its fruit each month; and the leaves of the tree were for the healing of the nations.

◆ ***Poem*** by Rabindranath Tagore, *from* **This Year of Grace**

In the music of the rushing stream sounds the joyful assurance I shall become the sea. It is not vain assumption, it is true humility, for it is the truth. The river has no other alternative. On both sides of the bank it has numerous fields and forests, villages and towns, it can serve them in various ways, cleanse them and feed them, carry their produce to place by place.

But it can have only partial relations with them and however long it may linger among them it remains separate, it can never become a town or a forest.

But it can and does become the sea. The lesser moving water has its affinity with the great motionless water of the ocean, it moves through the thousand objects on its outward course and the motion finds its finality when it reaches the sea.

◆ ***The River*** by Dorothea Eastwood

What the water sang
I could never exactly hear;
Of sleep and dreams, I thought, the knell
Of Time, the passing of each lovely thing
Between spring and spring.
But I thought too, it told of Life
That brings to birth
With no less certainty
Between spring and spring
The immortal and heavenly here on earth.
But the final truth I never heard quite right.
Perhaps no man could;
Only the willows, the wild duck and the reeds,
Things that listen quietly,
Night after night.

◆ ***Poem*** by Alfred, Lord Tennyson

Flow down, cold rivulet, to the sea
    Thy tribute wave deliver:
No more by thee my steps shall be
    For ever and for ever.

Flow softly, flow, by lawn and lee
    A rivulet then a river:

No where by thee my steps shall be
For ever and for ever.

But here will sigh thine alder tree
And here thine aspen shiver,
And here by thee will hum the bee;
For ever and for ever.

A thousand suns will stream on thee
A thousand moons will quiver:
But not by thee my steps will be,
For ever and for ever.

◆ ***Composed upon Westminster Bridge*** by William Wordsworth, *taken from* **Miscellaneous Sonnets** Pt II XXXVI

Earth has not anything to show more fair:
Dull would he be of soul who could pass by
A sight so touching in its majesty:
This City now doth, like a garment, wear
The beauty of the morning; silent, bare,
Ships, towers, domes, theatres and temples lie
Open unto the fields, and to the sky;
All bright and glittering in the smokeless air.
Never did sun more beautifully steep
In his first splendour, valley, rock or hill;
Ne'er saw I, never felt, a calm so deep!
The river glideth at his own sweet will:
Dear God! the very houses seem asleep;
And all that mighty heart is lying still!

◆ ***The Listener*** by Walter De La Mare

Who is it calling by the darkened river
Where the moss lies smooth and deep,
And the dark trees lean unmoving arms,
Silent and vague in sleep,
And the bright-heeled constellations pass
In splendour through the gloom;

Who is it calling o'er the darkened river
In music, 'Come . . .'?

Who is it wandering in the summer meadows
Where the children stoop and play
In the green faint-scented flowers, spinning
The guileless hours away?
Who touches their bright hair? Who puts
A wind shell to each cheek,
Whispering betwixt its breathing silences,
'Seek, Seek . . .'?

Who is it watching in the gathering twilight
When the curfew bird hath flown
On eager wings, from song to silence,
To its darkened nest alone?
Who takes for brightening eyes the stars,
For locks the still moonbeams,
Sighs through the dews of evening peacefully
Falling, 'Dreams . . .'?

## TREES

### OUR INHERITANCE

*So many of the trees I have known seem to portray the best characteristics of those who planted them.*

*The Beeches speak of those elegant patricians who have lived in their stately homes for century after century. I have been told that you could always tell the politics of the owners by their avenues. The Tories planted Beeches and the Whigs planted Limes.*

*The Oaks, 'the hearts of oak', speak of Great Britain, especially on the high seas; the famous Hatfield tree under which the young Princess was sitting when the news came of her sister Mary's death and she therefore became the first Queen Elizabeth; the Boscabel Oak which saved the life of the hunted King Charles II.*

*To stand within the shell of what remains of a giant, age-old Oak tree will cause you to marvel at nature's sculpting of countless niches where*

*Rackham would have depicted tiny elves and fairies perching, ready to vanish from sight on one's intrusion on their privacy.*

*The great Lime avenues with their clumps of mistletoe hanging from their upper branches, far out of reach of the Christmas vandals, seem to speak of literary genius, possibly because the one I know best was where Jane Austen wrote many of her books.*

*The Scots Pines make one think of those hardy, dignified Scots who have settled in all parts of the world and taken with them their gallant, stalwart loyalty to the country of their birth and to all that they believe in.*

*The Willows remind one of quiet, peaceful, lazy summer days in the water meadows, or the sound of bat striking ball on the village green, breaking the silence, or of the weeping of those who have lost someone they love. Somehow one feels these trees must all have a way of communicating with each other and with us. I so much like Ted Hughes' idea in his poem 'A Wind flashes the Grass'.*

> *'And the incomprehensible cry*
> *From the boughs in the wind*
> *Sets us listening for below words.'*

◆ *From* **Selected Poems 1957–1981** by Ted Hughes

A WIND FLASHES THE GRASS

Leaves pour blackly across
We cling to the earth, with glistening eyes, pierced
    afresh by the trees' cry
And the incomprehensible cry
From the boughs in the wind
Sets us listening for below words,
Meanings that will not part from the rock.

The trees thunder in unison, on a gloomy afternoon
And the ploughman grows anxious, his tractor becomes
    terrible
His memory litters downwind
And the shadow of his bones tosses darkly on the air.

The trees suddenly storm to a stop, in a hush
Against the sky, where the field ends

They crowd there shuddering
And wary, like horses bewildered by lightning.

The stirring of their twigs against the dark,
travelling sky
Is the oracle of the earth.

They too are afraid they too are momentary
Streams, rivers of shadow.

◆ ***Parochial and Plain Sermons*** by John Henry Newman

Once only in the year, yet once does the world which we see show forth its hidden powers, and in a manner manifest itself.

Then the leaves come out, and the blossoms on the fruit trees and flowers and the grass and corn spring up. There is a sudden rush and burst outwardly of the hidden life which God has lodged in the material world. Well that shows you as by a sample what it can do at God's command. When he gives the word. This earth which now buds forth in leaves and blossoms, will one day burst forth into a new world of light and glory, in which we shall see saints and angels dwelling. Who would think, except from his experience of former springs all through his life, who would conceive two or three months before, that it was possible that the face of nature, which then seemed so lifeless, should become so splendid and varied? So it is with the coming of that eternal Spring for which all Christians are waiting. Come it will, though it delay, yet though it tarry, let us wait for it, 'because it will surely come, it will not tarry'. Therefore we say day by day, Thy Kingdom come, which means, 'O Lord show thyself, manifest thyself; stir up thy strength, thou that sittest between the cherubim, show thyself, stir up thy strength and come and help us' (Psalm 80). The earth that we see does not satisfy us. What we see is the outward shell of an eternal kingdom and on that kingdom we fix the eyes of faith.

Shine forth, O Lord, as when on thy nativity thy angels visited the shepherds, let thy glory blossom forth as bloom and foliage on the trees. Bright as is the sun, and the sky and the clouds, green as are the leaves and the fields, sweet as is the singing of the birds. We know that they are not all, and we will not take up with a part for the whole.

They proceed from a centre of love and goodness, which is God himself, but they are not his fullness, they speak of heaven but they are not heaven, they are but as stray beams and dim reflections of his image, they are but the crumbs from the table.

*The next quotation, from* The Eye of the Eagle, *rings many bells for me. I was once trying to help a young man with his Arts Course for the Open University. One evening he brought back the lovely poem by Gerard Manley Hopkins, 'The Binsey Poplars', to study.*

*To my dismay he was being taught to dissect it word by word and phrase by phrase, presumably to learn the structure of poetry. For me this was like physically killing the poem. I felt it would never be quite the same, however carefully I put it together again.*

*I cannot help asking myself, is this the only way to teach the structure of poetry? Is there not a grave danger of destroying the God-given inspiration coming from the deep centre of our being?*

*It seems that the Celtic poets did not learn their 'structure' in this way. The author of* The Eye of the Eagle, *David Adam, writes: 'To dissect living things is fatal, we are always waiting to take things apart, to analyse.' In one sense poems are living things: they are part of the poet.*

*After reading Miss Jill Pirrie's fascinating book,* On Common Ground, *I would guess that the way in which she brings out the inner thoughts for her pupils is a far more satisfactory method.*

◆ *From* **The Eye of the Eagle** by David Adam

The Celtic Christians tended to seek to discover the underlying unity in all things rather than their separation, to align things rather than to divide them. Instead of looking at secondary causes of secondary causes they were concerned with the Prime Mover who united all. There was a consciousness of the integral wholeness in nature, an almost tender awareness of the unseen strands that unite all things.

So many of us have lost touch with reality and thus live in a fantasy world of distorted vision. In this distorted world one can be very alone. This restricted world is of our own making and not half as exciting as the real thing. What we need to do is to break out from this narrow myopic world and widen our vision. Let us be seen as those who extend horizons, those who reach beyond the stars, beyond the created universe to the Creator Himself, who gives meaning and being to all. Let us look into the very centre of things and discover the mystery that unites all. Let us forever in our looking at material things say 'Be thou my vision, O Lord'.

◆ ***The Binsey Poplars*** by Gerard Manley Hopkins

My aspens dear whose airy cages quelled,
Quelled or quenched in leaves the leaping sun.
All felled, felled, are all felled;
Of a fresh and following folded rank
Not spared, not one
That dandles and sandalled
Shadow that swam or sank

On meadow and river and wind-wandering weed-winding bank.

O if we but knew what we do
When we delve or hew –
Hack and rack the growing green.

Since country is so tender
To touch her being so slender,
That like this sleek and seeing ball
But a prick will make no eye at all,
Where we, even where we mean
To mind how we can hew
When we hew and delve;
After-comers cannot guess the beauty been

Ten or twelve, only ten or twelve
Strokes of havoc unselve
The sweet especial scene,
Sweet especial rural scene.

◆ *The Death Sentence* by Briony Verdon, aged twelve, *taken from* **On Common Ground: A Programme for Teaching Poetry** by Jill Pirrie

Tall straight pillars,
Huge great trees
Large, may be
But defenceless
Like children
Deserted by parents.
The axe swings
The tree falls
As a soldier in battle
But the tree has no mouth
To protest.
The tree has no legs
To run.
The tree has no gun
To take revenge.
For the sake of a table
A sheet of paper,
A cabinet,
Trees
Standing tall and dark
Large and menacing
But defenceless against
The lumberjack's axe.
One by one they fell
As soldiers in the battle
A forest full of life
Then nothing.

◆ *From* **School of Prayer** by Olive Wyon. Olive Wyon quotes from Johannes Ruysbroek.

When summer draws near and the sun rises higher, it draws the moisture out of the earth through the roots and through the trunks of the trees into the twigs and hence foliage, flowers and fruit. So, likewise when Christ the eternal sun rises and shines in our hearts so that it is summer, He gives His light and His heat to our desires and draws the heart from the multiplicity of earthly things and brings about unity and inwardness and makes the heart grow and bring forth the leaves, the flowers of ardent devotion and the fruits of thanksgiving and praise.

◆ *From* **Poetry in the Making** by Ted Hughes

Here is a poem about almond trees in Sicily in winter, by D. H. Lawrence. He has extremely interesting thoughts about almond trees and just see how he twines them round his trees – but the trees are always there, he never loses sight of them.

BARE ALMOND TREES

Wet almond trees, in the rain
Like iron sticking grimly out of the earth;
Black almond trunks, in the rain,
Like iron implements, twisted, hideous out of
the earth,
Out of the deep, soft fledge of Sicilian
winter-green,
Earth-grass uneatable.
Almond trunks curving blackly, iron dark, climbing
the slopes.

Almond trees, beneath the terrace rail,
Black, rusted, iron trunk,
You have welded your thin stems finer,
Like steel, like sensitive steel in the air,
Grey, lavender, sensitive steel, curving thinly and
brittly up in a parabola.

What are you doing in the December rain?
Have you a strange electric sensitiveness in your
steel tips?
Do you feel the air for electric influences
Like some strange magnetic apparatus
Do you take in messages, in some strange code,
From heaven's wolfish, wandering electricity, that
prowls so constantly round Etna?

Do you take the whisper of sulphur from the air?
Do you hear the chemical accents of the sun?
Do you telephone the roar of the waters over the
 earth?
And from all this do you make calculations?
Sicily, December's Sicily in a mass of rain
With iron branching blackly, rusted like old, twisted
 implements
And brandishing and stooping over earth's wintry
 fledge, climbing the slopes
Of uneatable soft green!

*The following quotation from* The Secret Garden *I heard as part of a meditation given by Sister Denzil of the Community of St Andrews.*

*To illustrate her talk she had collected various items from nature such as a leaf, a twig, a flower, and a stone. We were asked to choose one in particular and then to meditate upon it and to say what had come into our minds.*

*I chose a tiny, round fir cone. All its segments had opened up to release the seeds into the ground and it seemed to me to be a very vivid example of the world, the tiny bracts being the hard times, the spaces in between the deep moments of peace and happiness, the whole being a minute, self-contained world of its own, perfectly fashioned and able to reproduce itself given the right environment.*

*It made me think of Julian of Norwich's hazelnut which she held in her hand, becoming aware that it contained everything.*

◆ *From* **The Sign of the Tree**

THE SECRET GARDEN

We should let nature invade and permeate our lives, for nature refines and educates our senses and prepares us to experience a reality, another world beyond her. But we are one with this other world and when we touch and enjoy elemental nature we strengthen our humanity and our sympathetic bond with material creation.

We should let ourselves be touched and moved by natural symbols. They point the way to the sacred.

. . . Each symbol, no matter how elemental, opens a window on a reality immensely larger than itself. And these symbols help us to grasp the essence of 'world'. Any tree, for example, is the tree of life and is one of the symbols mankind has used in an attempt to describe the nature and origin of our world.

Each elemental object exceeds what the senses can describe, it is a vehicle of mystery and the incarnate presence of the holy. Any natural object can represent the sacred, guarantee its presence and evoke worship.

. . . Grace is hidden in these veiled natural symbols. Through them the present may open for a fleeting moment into the infinity of God.

We cannot comprehend this, much less define it, but we can grasp intuitively that it is through the natural symbols that God conveys truths to us about Himself and about life.

◆ *From* **Mysticism** by Evelyn Underhill

THE AWAKENING OF THE SELF

The use of visible nature as the stuff of ontological perceptions, the medium whereby nature as the self reaches out to the Absolute, is not rare in the history of mysticism. The mysterious vitality of trees, the silent magic of the forest, the strange and steady cycle of its life, possess in a peculiar degree this power of unleashing the human soul; are curiously friendly to its cravings, minister to its inarticulate needs. Unsullied by the corroding touch of consciousness, that life can make contact with the 'great life of All'; and through its mighty rhythms man can receive a message concerning the true and timeless 'World of all' that is, and was, and evermore shall be.

◆ *From* **Touch the Earth – A Self-Portrait of Indian Existence**. Compiled by T.C. McLuhan

'The great care with which so many of the Indians utilised every portion of the carcass of a hunted animal,' writes Dorothy Lee, an anthropologist, 'was an expression not of economic thrift, but of courtesy and respect; in fact an aspect of the religious relationship to the slain.' The Wintu Indians of California lived on very dense wooded land where it was difficult even to find clear land to erect houses. 'Nevertheless,' continues Lee, 'they would use only dead wood for fuel, out of respect for nature.' In the following passage, an old holy Wintu woman speaks sadly about the needless destruction of the land in which she lived – a place where gold mining and particularly hydraulic mining had torn up the earth.

'The white people never cared for land or deer or bear. When we Indians build houses, we make little holes. When we burn grass for grasshoppers, we don't ruin things. We shake down acorns and pinenuts. We don't chop down the trees. We only use dead wood. But the white people plow up the ground, pull down the trees, kill everything. The tree says, "Don't, I am sore. Don't hurt me." But they chop it down and cut it up. The spirit of the land hates them. They blast out trees and stir it up to its depths. They saw up the trees; that hurts them.'

◆ *From* **Who Thought of the Lilac?** by Humbert Wolfe 1885–1940, found in **Gardens of the Mind**

THE LILAC

Who thought of the lilac?
'I' dew said,
'I made the lilac
out of my head.'

'She made the lilac'.
'Pooh!' trilled the linnet,
and each dew note had a
lilac in it.

◆ *From* **Touch the Earth**. Compiled by T.C. McLuhan

TATANGE MANI. 1811

We were lawless people, but we were on pretty good terms with the Great Spirit, creator and ruler of all. You whites assumed we were savages. You didn't understand our prayers. You didn't try to understand. When we sang our praises to the sun or moon or wind, you said we were worshipping idols. Without understanding you condemned us as lost souls just because our form of worship was different to yours.

We saw the Great Spirit's work in almost everything, sun, moon, trees, wind and mountains. Sometimes we approached him through these things. Was that so bad? I think we have a true belief in the supreme being, a stronger faith than that of most of the whites who have called us pagans . . . Indians living close to nature and nature's rules are not living in darkness.

Did you know that trees talk? Well, they do. They talk to each other, and they'll talk to you if you listen. Trouble is white people don't listen. They never learned to listen to the Indians so I don't suppose they'll listen to other voices in Nature. But I have learned a lot from trees: sometimes about the weather, sometimes about animals, sometimes about the Great Spirit.

◆ *From* **A Thousand Reasons for Living** by Dom Helder Camara

I love looking at you
hundred year old tree,
loaded with shoots and boughs
as though you were a stripling.
Teach me the secret
of growing old like you
open to life, to youth, to decay
as somebody aware
that youth and age
are merely steps
towards eternity.

◆ *From* **The Sacred Pipe**: Black Elk's account of the Seven Rites of the Oglala Sioux

Perhaps it may be and this is my prayer, that through our sacred pipe peace may come to those people who understand, an understanding which must be of the heart and not of the head alone. Then they will realize that we Indians know the One True God and that we pray to Him continually.

We should understand well that all things are the works of the Great Spirit. We should know that He is within all things: the trees, the grasses, the rivers, the mountains and all four-legged animals and the winged peoples; and even more important, we should understand all this deeply in our hearts, then we will be and act and live as He intends.

◆ ***Disclosure*** by Ann Lewin from The Christian Meditation Centre

Prayer is like watching for the
Kingfisher. All you can do is
Be where he is likely to appear and
Wait.
Often nothing much happens,
There is space, silence and
Expectancy.
No visible sign, only the
Knowledge that he's been there
And may come again.
Seeing or not seeing cease to matter,
You have been prepared.
But when you've almost stopped
Expecting it, a flash of brightness
Gives encouragement.

◆ 3 ◆

# The Journey
# The Ongoing Revelation

## THE JOURNEY

*In our journey through life, the spiritual dimension must not be neglected. For me I think that it has been after some great sorrow that the importance of this has become deepened and paramount.*

*When things go well it is so easy to live on the surface, to take things for granted, but in sorrow and loss the breakthrough to a deeper reality takes over. Probably not at once, but gradually, the sorrow leads to a deepening of faith and the determination to see that somehow this tragedy must bring something positive and creative out of what has seemed totally negative and destructive – something which brings meaning to meaninglessness.*

*This chapter, the Journey, the pilgrimage, takes in the inspiration of those who have been through the depths and have found there this other dimension, through other people, through nature, through music, through the joys and sorrows of life, through other faiths and through their own faith in God.*

*Throughout our journey we shall inevitably encounter people of other faiths, people who think differently about the things that really matter to us all, people who are travelling by different routes to those which we have chosen, or which have been chosen for us.*

*In this chapter I have included quotations from those who have really studied at depth this difficult question of how we should react without seeming to be disloyal to our own commitment to Christ and all which that entails. I offer them with great humility in the realisation that I myself can only claim an appreciation of the seriousness of this problem and no real knowledge as to how it can be resolved.*

*I believe with Hans Kung that 'there can never be peace in the world until there is peace between the religions of the world'.*

*Surely the dialogue must be encouraged and not condemned.*

*From a letter in* The Friend

*Youth is not a time of life; it is a state of mind. It is the freshness of the deep springs of life. No one grows old merely by living a number of years. People grow old by deserting their ideals. Whether they are sixty or sixteen, every human being may experience wonder – the undaunted challenge of events, the unfailing appetite for the future, the joy in living.*

*For you are as young as your faith, or as old as your doubts.*

*As long as your heart receives messages of beauty, hope, cheer, courage and power from God and your fellow men, you are young.*

◆ *From* **Anglican Spirituality: A Continuing Tradition** by William Purcell

THE PATH WITHIN

'Patches of God – light in the woods of our experience.' So C.S. Lewis spoke of what can be encountered through prayer and contemplation.

This is the path within, that part of the spiritual life which takes the individual into the secret places of the soul.

Spirituality is a pilgrimage which takes us through the world towards God. It is a journey which crosses different kinds of country, and the pilgrim may be required to traverse them all from time to time.

There is the route through the outer world, where the concern must be with trying to live a God-focused life among the challenges of every day.

There is a spirituality of social action, properly so described because it is motivated by beliefs about God and the world and the need in many particular actions to try to make it a better one in his name.

◆ *From* **The Sanskrit**, author and translator unknown

LOOK TO THIS DAY

Look to this day. For it is life, the very life of life. In its brief course lie all the varieties and realities of your existence: the bliss of growth, the glory of action, the splendour of beauty. For yesterday is already a dream, and tomorrow is only a vision, but today well lived makes every yesterday a dream of happiness, and every tomorrow a vision of hope.

Look well, therefore, to this day! Such is the salutation of the dawn.

◆ *From* **Walk to Jerusalem** by Gerard Hughes

The mystic sees into the heart of things, her vision is not limited to time or space. Her awful vision is being realised in our own day. The roots of our destructiveness are in the human heart.

Thus
humankind does well to keep honesty
to keep to truth.

Those that love lies
bring suffering
not only to themselves
but to others as well
since they are driven to ever more lies.

Their lies are like the juiceless foam,
hard and black,
lacking the verdancy of justice
it is dry,
totally without illuminating virtue.

As often as the elements of the world
are violated
by ill treatment
so God will cleanse them
God will cleanse them
through the sufferings
through the hardships.

◆ *From* **Gitanjali** by Rabindranath Tagore

XIII

The time that my journey takes is long and the way of it is long.

I came out on the chariot of the first gleam of light, and pursued my voyage through the wilderness of worlds leaving my track on many a star and a planet.

It is the most distant course that comes nearest to Thyself, and that training is the most intricate which leads to the utter simplicity of a tune.

The traveller has to knock at every alien door to come to his own, and one has to wander through all the outer worlds to reach the innermost shrine at the end.

My eyes strayed far and wide before I shut them and said 'Here art thou.'

The question and the cry 'Oh where?' melt in tears of a thousand streams and deluge the world with the flood of assurance.

(I AM.)

◆ ***The Simplicity of Prayer*** by Mother Mary Clare SLG

We must try to understand
the meaning of the age
in which we are called to bear witness.
We must accept the fact
this is an age in which
the cloth is being unwoven.
It is therefore no good trying
to patch. We must, rather,
set up the loom on which
coming generations may
weave new cloth according to
the pattern God provides.

◆ *From* **Walk to Jerusalem** by Gerard Hughes

God is a living reality, not a concept, and we meet him, not through uttering a creed, but in the way we live and relate to one another, to ourselves and to all creation. Those who hunger and thirst after justice, hunger and thirst for God, no matter what their faith or ideology may be. If they care for their neighbour as they care for themselves, then they are meeting God, even if they do not know, or even if they deny his name. Therefore for Catholic or for any other Christians to say, 'Before we can work together for justice and peace on earth, we must first settle our doctrines, or ethical, or political differences', is a long-winded way of saying, 'We cannot work together for justice and peace', or 'We are unwilling to do so'.

When we reach heaven we shall discover that many people called 'unbelievers', 'communists' or 'humanists' have entered the kingdom of God before those who have prided themselves on their Christian orthodoxy and who, locked in their exclusive righteousness, have contributed nothing to justice and peace, but only fostered division.

◆ ***Goethe***

The moment one definitely commits oneself, then providence moves too. All sorts of things occur to help one that would never otherwise have occurred.

A whole stream of events issues from the decision, raising in one's favour all manner of unforeseen incidents and meetings and material assistance which no man could have dreamed would have come his way.

Whatever you can do or dream you can, begin it. Boldness has genius, power and magic in it.

◆ ***Evelyn Waugh*** *from* **In Pursuit of Happiness** by Richard Harries

'God wants a different thing from each one of us, laborious or easy, conspicuous or quite private, but something which only we can do and for which we were created.'

This is a bold and startling claim. Yet it is not idiosyncratic. Here are some words of Newman (which could perhaps underline the passage of Waugh).

'God has created me to do him some definite service. He has committed one work to me which he has not committed to another.

'I have my mission. I have a part in a great work. I am a link in a chain, a bond of connection between persons. He has not created me for naught. I shall do his work.'

◆ ***Faith*** by E.B.

*Our Christian Faith is that God revealed Himself to us in the life of Jesus Christ. If we believe this;*

*if we believe that God created the world and everything in it;*

*if we believe God's word, 'before Abraham was, I AM';*
*if we believe in the Trinity, God, Christ and the Holy Spirit;*
*if we believe in the Resurrection and all that entails and in the sending of the Holy Spirit, the Comforter to dwell within each one of us –*
*then how can we not believe that God with Christ and the Holy Spirit are not everywhere in His world, in every human soul; revealed in some way to men of other faiths, through their prophets, their holy men, their belief in a transcendence above and beyond themselves?*

*I realise that some dedicated Christians will look askance at this suggestion, because they believe that salvation is restricted to the Christian religion. But this I can't accept.*

*I think of an elderly Hindu who, after listening to a talk about Christ, came to the speaker and said, 'Thank you. I have known Him all my life and now you have told me His name'.*

*I once read of a nun who, while driving in India with a visiting bishop, passed a Hindu shrine by the roadside. This was surrounded with offerings of flowers, fruit and other gifts.*

*'How sad,' she remarked. 'They don't know that there is no one there.' To my mind, of course, God was there to receive those humble, loving offerings. Could it have been that it was purely her own* image *of God which was absent? Perhaps she herself was unaware of the universality of God and Christ present to the worshippers at the shrine who, in their giving, were showing their love and gratitude to the supreme being in the only way they knew.*

◆ *From* **Letters of Direction** by the Abbé De Tourville

FORERUNNERS

In every age God has scattered forerunners in the world. They are those who are ahead of their time and whose personal action is based on an inward knowledge of that which is to come. If you and I should happen to be forerunners, let us bless God for it, even though, living a century or two too soon, we may feel ourselves to be strangers in a foreign land.

Rejoice then in the light which you have been given and do not be surprised that it is so difficult to pass it on to others . . . It really is making its way, not so much through you or me as through force of circumstances. You are simply ahead of your time; it is a good thing to have long sight and to let your soul be illumined as soon as you are aware of that light.

Intelligent people can no longer deceive themselves about old systems and old ideas, circumstances have radically changed and changed beyond possibility of recall. Such people are in just the same situation as yourself. It is a situation which often seems hard but is in reality infinitely less hard than the contrary situation would be. For that would mean living a falsehood and driving into falsehood new generations who would be bound to suffer even more than we ourselves.

Be open to all new ideas and be glad to put them into practice wherever, as far as your understanding of people goes, it is practicable or possible.

◆ *From* **Inner Journey, Outer Journey** by James Roose-Evans

Many Christians, perhaps the majority, feel threatened by any religious tradition other than their own.

They cannot acknowledge, let alone perceive the wisdom and beauty of the Upanishads, the Sufi mystics, the writings of Lao Tsu, the teaching of the Hasid or of the Buddha, nor see how it is possible to be enriched by those insights and weave them into their own lives as Christians . . .

. . . The emergence of a global society has brought with it the idea that we must develop a new consciousness and identity as world citizens so that we need a new kind of world believer who can meaningfully relate to the perception of more than one religious tradition, and thereby find a deep enrichment.

There can be but one God under all, and one family of God. The truth shines with its own light. Each of us approaches the Eternal Reality along a particular path, cultural, geographical, biolographical. Recently Dom Bede Griffiths OSB, a Benedictine monk who for the past thirty years has lived in an ashram in India, remarked: 'To me the meeting of Western religions with the religions of the East is really one of the focal points of human development today. I do not feel that religions can go on simply following their own path separately. We have reached a point in evolution where we have to meet. We have to share, to discover one another.'

This is beginning to happen all over the world, so that a new kind of spirituality is starting to emerge. We are gradually seeing what unites rather than what divides.

In 1986 Pope Paul invited the leaders of the world religions to join him in Assisi to pray for world peace. 'I'll wait for you there,' was his simple message. 'Meet me there and we shall pray together.'

◆ ***Spreading the Gospel*** by E.B.

THE GOOD NEWS: SOWING THE SEED

*My personal feeling is that sowing the seed should be done very gently. Sowing the seed, planting the plant, has to be done lovingly and with great care, taking into consideration where the one you are talking to stands at that moment, remembering all the time that God is there in that other person.*

*He was there before you came; we need to be aware of this and to be careful, very careful not to trample on the seed or break off the shoot that is already beginning to grow.*

*I believe that the Gospel is spread more by what we are than by what we say or do. Words can be so divisive, so easily misunderstood or misrepresented, and, alas, so off-putting to the sensitive and perceptive recipient.*

*Of course, words are a necessary way of communication, we can hardly do without them, but as Canon Stancliffe once wrote, 'They should come out of silence. It is in silence that we learn what to say and how to say it.'*

> *O Lord give us the wisdom to know when to speak and when to hold our peace. Teach us to listen with our hearts as well as our ears, with true compassion, Thy compassion, giving space for thy Holy Spirit to speak through us.*
>
> *Amen.*

◆ *From* **The Gate of Healing** by Ian Pearce

Talk not to all about things sublime and essential.
Seek the level of him with whom you speak,
So as not to humble or distress him.
Be frivolous too when you are with the frivolous.
But once in a while, as if unsought or even
thoughtlessly

Drop into their cup on the foam of frivolity, a very
small petal from the flower of your dreams.
If it is not noticed, recover it courteously, and,
always smiling go on your way.

If, however, someone picks up the frail small petal, and
examines it, inhales its fragrance,
Give him forthwith and carefully, the sign of discreet
understanding.
Then let him behold one of the few marvellous flowers
of your garden.
Tell him of the invisible divinity which surrounds
us all
And give him of the invisible magic word, the open-sesame
to true freedom.

◆ ***Prayer*** by Bishop Ridding, taken from **Prayers for a Troubled Heart** by George Appleton

WHEN FAITH IS STRAINED

In times of doubt and questions, when our belief is perplexed by new teaching, new thought, when our faith is strained by creeds, by doctrines, by mysteries beyond our understanding, give us the faithfulness of learners, and the courage of believers in Thee; give us boldness to examine and faith to trust all truth, stability to hold fast our tradition with enlightened interpretation, to grasp new knowledge and combine it loyally and honestly with old; alike from stubborn rejection of new revelation and from hasty assurance that we are wiser than our Fathers, save us and help us, O Lord.

◆ *From* **the Easter Day Sermon** preached by Dr Robert Runcie in Canterbury Cathedral 1990

Anyone who has shared an Easter service in an Orthodox church in the dark days of Russia or Romania will know its powerful effect.

The devotion of the people packed together, over long hours, the candles passed from hand to hand light up deep lines of sorrow and tragedy on the faces behind them.

. . . Our experiences in Western Europe and especially in our own country have been very different. We have not faced persecution.

There has been no systematic attempt to erase the Christian faith or to destroy our Christian institutions. Our faith is tested in subtler ways. We do not face an open enemy in broad daylight.

Ours, in the words of John Henry Newman, is a night battle. It is sometimes hard to distinguish friend from foe. Atheism, materialism, secularism wear camouflage and are sometimes disguised as angels of light. Mockery and indifference can wear down our faith more effectively than harsh persecution. These tests of faith may not be so dramatic or clear-cut but they make the same demands on our spiritual resources.

They remind us that good and evil are never distinguished by lines on a map but in the words of Alexander Solzhenitsyn, 'The line separating good and evil passes not through states or between classes, nor between political parties . . . but right through every human heart and through all human hearts'.

Each of us must discover spiritual courage in the routines and crises of everyday life, each of us is faced with sickness, bereavement, disappointment, betrayal, anxiety. But in the darkest places is Christ's Easter light. C.S. Lewis wrote, 'I believe in Christianity as I believe the sun has risen not only because I see it, but because by it I see everything else'. Because Christ has risen, because he has promised eternal life to all who believe in Him, we look out on a world where despair never has the last word. And wherever we proclaim that Christ is risen walls come tumbling down, hope drives out despair, the impossible happens.

. . . In Him we find a new sense of freedom. In the Gospels faith is never set over against unbelief. It is always set over against fear. 'Why are you afraid?' our Lord says. 'Have you no faith?' Fear of others and of what others will think, fear and its consequences, fear of illness or inadequacy, fear of death. These are the tensions which dominate our lives.

When faith is really embraced and life handed over to the Lord himself then we know the beginning of Christian faith.

That freedom does not guarantee tranquillity, nor does it smooth the jagged edges of life's way. That is because the Christian faith does not end with the calming of the self-centred body or the achievement of an earthly utopia, but is a journey in the strength of cross and resurrection into the very life of heaven itself.

◆ *From* **The Universal Christ: Daily Readings with Bede Griffiths**

BEYOND RELIGION

It is no longer possible today for one religion to live in isolation from other religions. In almost every country people of different religions are meeting one another and being compelled to face their differences.

More and more the necessity for contact is being realized. Those who attempt to do so are feeling that dialogue when properly understood is not a compromise but a process of enrichment by which each religion opens itself to the truth to be found in the other religion, and the two parties grow together in a common desire for truth.

Each religion has to hold to its own tradition, yet to allow that tradition to grow as it opens itself to other aspects of truth . . .

So we realise that truth is one, but that it has many faces and each religion is an aspect of that face. The one truth is perceived to be manifesting itself under different signs and symbols.

◆ *From* **The Inner Christ** by John Main

There is a need for men and women who are not religious bigots, not intolerant of other religious men and women, but who are strong with the power of the Spirit and who know that it is a universal spirit of love.

We need Christian people who realise that we have nothing to fear from the Buddhist tradition or the Hindu tradition or any tradition that is truly spiritual.

We have only to learn how to see one another in the light of Christ. But this we can only do if we allow his light to burn not just brightly but brilliantly in our own hearts by standing back, getting out of the way so that the light of love, compassion and forgiveness may become supreme in our spirit.

◆ *From* **Prayer in a Troubled World** by George Appleton

O Spirit of God guide us
as we seek to discover thy working
with men of other faiths.
Give us the strength of truth,
the gentleness and strength of love,
the clear judgement, and the courage of faith.
Above all grant us a deep understanding
of him who is the truth,
a greater commitment to him who is the Lord,
a deeper gratitude to him
who is the Saviour of all,
even Jesus Christ thy Eternal Word,
through whom thou art drawing all men
that they may be saved for ever,
and worship thee the one God.
Amen.

◆ *From* **Forewords** by Marcus Braybrook

The God revealed in Jesus Christ is the one God of all people. Schubert Ogden has written, 'The New Testament sense of claim "only in Jesus Christ", is not that God is only to be found in Jesus and nowhere else, but that the only God who is to be found anywhere – though He is to be found everywhere – is the God who is made known in the word that Jesus speaks and is.' In Jesus the reality of God as loving Father is made known and wherever signs of God's activity are recognised, it will be one and the same God who is seen to be at work. Equally other insights will not be contrary to Christ although they may lead us to deeper understanding of Him.

The missionary C.F. Andrews, towards the end of his years in India, said that through his deep contact with members of other faiths, Christ had become not less central but more central and universal: 'not less divine but more so because more universally human'.

The Christian therefore gives full allegiance to Jesus as the One who has revealed self-giving, sacrificial love as the meaning of life: but will rejoice at every evidence of the universal self-revelation of God, and while witnessing to his own knowledge of God in Christ will learn from the testimonies of others.

For too long in misguided loyalty to Christ, Christians have cut themselves off from other religious communities. The pressure of the Spirit that has brought humankind together in our century in a new way prompts us to reach out hands of fellowship.

In partnership with others and in loyalty to Christ we shall seek those universal truths and values he embodied. In the words of a Hindu scholar, 'Jesus does not belong to the Church, we love him too'.

◆ *From* **The Vision of the Nazarene**, set down by the author of the Initiate

OF SECTS AND SECTARIANS

And the Radiant One led me into another church where a white-robed priest exhorted his listeners to provide money for the conversion of the heathen.

And again the Master smiled as He said,

'O My disciples, did I ever say, "Lo there is but one belief and one religion that is right and all others verily they are wrong"?

'Yet because I said to My disciples, "Go ye into the world and preach the good tidings," the unreflecting have misinterpreted My words and made of them a plea for wasteful and foolish deeds. For verily by this did I mean that each one should spread abroad My gospel of peace bringing comfort and enlightenment to his followers, because of love and kindness of heart, but not that Man should sow seeds of dissension and strife, arrogant in the conviction that he alone is right, all others wrong.

'Truly God is one, but by many names may He be called by His devotees: yet alas do My followers distress themselves much because of those other names. But to them would I say: "Ere ye condemn the religion of another, see to it also first that you understand that religion, and see to it also that ye understand your own religion: for in essence all are the same."

'O My disciples, not a matter of belief in conversion but a matter of the heart; and much do the reflecting seek to convert those who are already converted. But did I not say erewhile, I came not to destroy the law and the prophets but to fulfil them?

My followers seek to discountenance these older religions in spite of My words – and this because they have lost the understanding of the Law and the Prophets.

'Verily all religions are One, and he who worships the Father worships Brahman, and he who worships Brahman worships Tao for all those are but the various names for Love – Existence – and Bliss Absolute which in truth are God. Unity did I preach, for what greater unity could there be than to love thy neighbour as thyself? And hence sympathy and understanding did I preach – feeling *with* and for understanding *with* – for these truly are the children of love.

'But in spite of My saying, "By this shall all men know that ye are My disciples if ye have love one for another," yet have My followers been guilty of religious intolerance and have worked not together in unity and fellowship but in separate communities, one reviling the other.

'And now learn, O My Brother Beloved, Truth is infinite, although it is One and not in this or that sect, or in this or that book is all Truth contained.

'Nevertheless to the selfless of heart shall Truth be revealed.'

◆ *From* **Bread of the World** by John Hadley

The past and the present need to meet through the study of Christian history, and attention to the writings we have inherited.

But finally (if anything can be final), we cannot confine the Spirit to the human boundaries of the Church or the Christian religion. If our faith is to live and grow, we must talk and listen to people from other fields and other faiths, to poets and philosophers, sociologists and politicians, mathematicians and astrologers, all who work and think at the frontiers of human knowledge and experience, to people of other religions than our own, those who come at God from a different angle, and those for whom God appears only as darkness.

◆ *From* **Letters of Direction** by the Abbé De Tourville

Rejoice that you are what you are, for our Lord loves you very dearly. He loves the whole of you, just as you are. In spite therefore of all your troubles, troubles about people and things remain at peace. Drop all your spiritual anxieties and do not goad yourself to efforts which will only over-burden and over-strain you. Such efforts are not only useless but even harmful, for they war against that peace which, in this world, must always exist in the midst of our imperfections, the imperfections of things, the imperfections of people. Imitate the calm of the sailor standing on the deck of his ship, which is in itself never still, or that of the man who walks quietly through the city, indifferent to noise and the winding of the streets, picking his way through the people and the traffic.

◆ *From* **Bread of the World** by John Hadley

SINGING THE LORD'S SONG IN A STRANGE LAND

It has always been painful to 'sing the Lord's song in a strange land'; a considerable portion of our GLORIA needs to be in the minor key.

It is painful to sing 'peace on earth' in a world like ours; if we sing it with our hearts, we shall be wounded by the contrast between the peace we sing, for which we long, and the terrible unpeacefulness that surrounds and invades us. But to sing 'peace on earth', is not just to express a wild hope or a vain longing, our song must in the end spill over from liturgy into life, so that our life itself in turn becomes a song of peace – and that will always be a hard song to sing.

For our Christian life – like the life of Jesus – is set between this peace which we sing, the song of the angels and the cross of the world's grimness; a tension that issues equally in pain and singing, as we hear so clearly in musical traditions like the Negro spirituals; and the harmonies of the Russian Church. It would be so much easier to let go of one pole or other, to forget God's glory and accept the grain of the world, or to concentrate gnostically on the spiritual realms, letting the things of the world grow strangely dim. But we must hold on to both, allowing the current of pain and glory to flow through us and out in almost unbearable melody, living and singing the tension between the sinful world and the song of its Creator.

As the psalmist says, 'Seeing the glory of God in the face of Jesus Christ'.

◆ *From* **A Journey to Ladakh** by Andrew Harvey

In the old days
In the old days of Shey
Everyone wore brocade of dragons.
And danced like peacocks.

In the old days
In the old days of Shey
Everyone wore shawls of silk
And belts of pure sheepswool.

'This song refers to the time,' Nawang said, 'when the kings of Ladakh lived at Shey. You must have seen the ruins of the Castle of Shey by the gompa. It is one of the saddest sights in Ladakh – Those great walls against the sky . . . The time is coming soon when anyone who sings this song will not know what the song is referring to, what the old dancers looked like, with their silk shawls and belts of sheepswool. Or if they do know, it will be only a kind of museum knowledge, or because troupes of dancers have been supported by tourist agencies.' He began to sing again.

I had a dream last night
I had a beautiful dream
I had a dream
In which all my hopes were fulfilled.

I saw a great iron bridge
Being built over the sea
I saw a garland of jewels
Floating on the water.

Taking up your sleeves my friends
Turn gently to the right
Winding your woollen shawls
Turn gently to the left.

May the young men of the village
Grow strong as Tigers
May the men of Tsangra village
Live free and strong as Tigers.

May the young women of the village
Grow like corn in Summer
May the young women of the village
Grow shining in the sun like the corn.

'It is hard not to feel bitter, singing that song now. How can I sing the first verse without feeling anger at what is being done to my people? What dreams for their future could I have that had any hope of being fulfilled? The great iron bridge built over the sea is the Buddhist faith, and the sea is the sea of Samsara . . . will Buddhism last in these mountains? Can the young men grow like Tigers under Kashmiri domination? Will the young women grow like shining corn when their innocence is gone?'

We sat silently. Nawang's sadness was too deep and too clear to be touched by anything but silence.

Then Nawang pointed across the mountains that were shining in the afternoon light, and said, 'There are so many songs to the light in Ladakh. The light is our real King. Without the light day after day I think I would have despaired long ago.'

◆ *From* **A Journey to Ladakh** by Andrew Harvey

'No society, no country, no world has a monopoly of spiritual insight, of spiritual truth. At this time of danger we all, Buddhists and Christians and atheists alike should share all the awareness we have, all the compassion we can find in ourselves, build up every possibility of goodwill that exists within us towards the world. I am a Tibetan Buddhist, but I am also, first and foremost, a man, and a man of my time, concerned for my time and for the establishment of peace and truth.'

◆ ***A Song My Lord to Thee*** by Brian Graham, *from* **The Review**

I am a candle, my Lord
Lit by your eternal flame,
Burn brightly in my yearning heart
In storm, in wind, in rain.

I am a river, my Lord
Flowing to the sea.
Direct me on my winding course
As I return to Thee.

I am a tree, my Lord
Growing beneath your sky,
Make me strong yet yielding
With roots that deeply lie.

I am a star, my Lord
Shining in the black of the night.
And to the weary traveller
May I give your light.

I am a human being, my Lord
I stumble and fall,
Help me to get up again
And follow your loving call.

◆ *From* **George MacDonald's Autobiography**

This story may not be just as the Lord told it, and yet may contain as its mirror as much of the truth as we are able to receive, and as will afford us scope for a life's discovery. The modifying influence of the human channels may be essential to God's revealing mode.

◆ *From* **The Diary of Pope John XXIII**

MY SOUL IN THESE PAGES . . .

'O my God make me love you and I shall be humble, make me love you more and I shall be humbler still.

O Jesus you must look after me a little too.

If all men are in the likeness of God why should I not love them all? Why should I despise them? Should I not rather revere them? This is the reflection which must hold me back from in any way offending against my brothers, for I must remember that they are all made in the image of God and that perhaps their souls are more beautiful and dearer to God than my own.

So a Divine hand has traced for me the path that leads to the Altar, seclusion, prayer and work. To pray working to work praying.'

Praying your life and living your prayer.

'And then I have noticed another thing. How is it that after I have been talking to someone for a long time even without meaning to show myself in a good light, I think it over and am depressed and discouraged? It is pride weeping over pride: crocodile tears. The fact that the more I speak about myself the more virtue I lose; vanity squirts out of every word, even from those which seem most innocent. I must get into my head that when I am with others, my fellows or my superiors, the best thing I can do is to preserve a becoming silence, or say only what is necessary or opportune; at least never to speak about myself unless I am interrogated and even then to say little and try to hold my listener's attention.'

◆ *From* **The Atlantis Log**, source unknown

Let me do my work each day, and if the darkened hour of despair overcome me, may I not forget the strength that comforted me in the desolation of other times. May I still remember the bright hours that found me walking over the silent hills of my childhood, or dreaming on the margin of the quiet river when a light glowed within me, and I promised my early God to have courage amid the tempests of the changing years.

Spare me from the bitterness and from the sharp passions of unguarded moments. May I not forget that poverty and riches are of the spirit. Though the world knows me not, may my thoughts and actions be such as shall keep me friendly with myself.

Lift my eyes from the earth and let me not forget the uses of the stars. Forbid that I should judge others lest I condemn myself. Let me not follow in the clamour of the world, but walk calmly in my path. Give me a few friends who will love me for what I am, and keep ever burning before my vagrant steps the kindly light of hope. And though age and infirmity overtake me, and I come not within the castle of my dreams, teach me still to be thankful for life and time's golden memories that are good and sweet – and may life's twilight find me gentle still.

◆ *From* **Uncommon Prayers**, collected by Cecil Hunt

By all means use some times to be alone!
Salute thyself! See what thy soul doth wear.

◆ ***Prayer***, attributed to Aby Behr, 527–634, father-in-law of Muhammad and first Caliph of Islam

I thank Thee, Lord, for knowing me better than I know myself and for letting me know myself better than others know me.

Make me, I pray Thee, better than they suppose, and forgive me what they do not know.

◆ **Henry Longfellow** *from* **Uncommon Prayers**, collected by Cecil Hunt

Oh blessed Lord! How much I need
Thy light to guide me on my way!
So many hands, that without heed,
Still touch Thy wounds and make them bleed.
So many feet that day by day
Still wander from Thy fold astray!
Feeble at best is my endeavour!
I see but cannot reach the height
That lies for ever in the Light;
And yet for ever and for ever,
When seeming just within my grasp,
I feel my feeble hands unclasp,

And sink discouraged into night;
For Thine own purpose Thou hast sent
The strife and the discouragement.

*I once heard Father Michael Hollings speak at a Quiet Day, which lives in my memory. In the few notes I managed to take were the following words. They may not have been exactly word for word as he said them, but I think this is the essence of what he said:*

*'You dare not condemn. The ultimate sin is hurting another person. I can still be morally right and yet cruel and unloving to others.*

*'As you grow older you cannot be judgemental. Judgementalism can be more dangerous than permissiveness. It was the Pharisees and the Sadducees who crucified our Lord. The way to heaven takes you through large tracts of fall. What is most important is the cleansing of the soul of judgementalism.' E.B.*

*O Lord, we all have so many friends who are in deep distress for one reason or another.*

*We are anxious about so many things, so many people. O Lord God, deepen and strengthen our trust in You for them and show us if there is any way in which we may be enabled to help them.*

*Hold them in Thy love and keep them in Thy remembrance.*
*For the sake of Jesus Christ our Lord and theirs, Amen. E.B.*

◆ ***To A Villain*** by Virginia Thesiger

How can I love you, young man
when I read of the things you have done,
when I look at your dissolute face
staring at me from the papers.

Let me first cleanse my heart of the pain,
let me first empty my mind of the horror,
let there be God and nothing but God
in my thought let there be peace.

Then I can look at your face and love
the man that is really you,
the man God made in the image and likeness
of all that is good and true.

Love, God's love is not anodyne
but active, powerful and strong:
like a sword, young man it will cut out your sin
and into the wound pour pity and hope.

And love, more love, that spreads like a tide
to comfort the hearts of those you have harmed,
and me and the world who look at your face
staring at us from the papers.

Love knows no barriers, frontiers, blocks
Love knows no sinner or sinned against.
God, let me latch on to love and the lovely
Let me be blessed and bless.

◆ *From* **A Wound Deep in the Heart** by Jean Vanier

TALK DURING UNITY WEEK, 1991

Jesus tells us: 'Do not be afraid of your own weakness. At the heart of your fragility, you will discover the presence of God. Be still, and within the wound of your loneliness you will find the friend, the divine friend.'

At the centre of the wound lies the mystery of the Cross and the resurrection, the mystery of a real presence, the presence of eternal life.

Here is the wisdom of Jesus Christ. We do not need to run away from our weakness or our loneliness but to discover in it the mystery, a mystery of forgiveness, of compassion and of presence.

◆ *From* **Complete Poems** by D.H. Lawrence

SHADOWS

And if tonight my soul may find her peace
In sleep, and sink in good oblivion,
And in the morning wake like a new-opened flower
Then I have been dipped again in God, and new-created.

And if weeks go round, in the dark of the moon
My spirit darkens and goes out, and soft strange gloom
pervades my movements and my thoughts and words
then I shall know that I am walking still
with God, we are close together now the moon's in shadow.
And if, as autumn deepens and darkens
I feel the pain of falling leaves, and stems that break in storm
and trouble and dissolution and distress
and then the softness of deep shadows folding, folding
around my soul and spirit, around my lips
so sweet, like a swoon, or more like the drowse of a low, sad
song
singing darker than the nightingale, on, on to the solstice
and the silence of short days, the silence of the year, the shadow,
then I shall know that my life is moving still
with the dark earth, and drenched
with the deep oblivion of earth's lapse and renewal.

And if in the changing phase of man's life
I fall in sickness and in misery
my wrists seem broken and my heart seems dead
and strength is gone, and my life
is only the leavings of a life
and still, among it all, snatches of lovely oblivion and snatches of
renewal
odd wintry flowers upon the withered stem, yet new, strange
flowers
such as my life has not brought forth before, new blossoms of
me –

then I shall know that still

I am in the hands of the unknown God,
he is breaking me down to his own oblivion
to send me forth on a new morning, a new man.

◆ *From* **The Eye of the Eagle** by David Adam

When we seek out the core of our existence, if we are not to become self-centred we need to continue our seeking until we come to God Himself. I know I must not give up until I come to the great Heart of my own heart. Then I will discover that I am in fact in the heart of God. My love may be small and vacillating, but His love for me is great and sure. I will learn that I have always been in my Father's house and heart, and that He has been looking for me with an everlasting love. Life is no longer full of *Angst* which distorts and disturbs my vision. Through the heart relationship the vision is cleared and all things seem to speak of God. Through the heart being receptive God is able to approach us through all His creation.

A CELTIC PRAYER

Bless to me, O God, the moon that is above me.
Bless to me, O God, the earth that is beneath me.
Bless to me, O God, my wife and my children.
Bless to me, O God, myself who have the care of them.

Bless, O God, the thing on which my eye doth rest.
Bless, O God, the thing on which my hope doth rest.
Bless, O God, my reason and my purpose.
Bless, O bless Thou them, Thou God of life.

◆ *From* **Bread of the World** by John Hadley

SENDING

When we are told to go out [*after Communion*] it means more than going out from the service and the building. It means – as it meant to the Apostles – going out from the safeness of the church into the dangerousness of the world; from the security of a nice Christian surrounding into the great secular insecurity that surrounds us, where everything will be questioned and nothing taken for granted. And we can, if we like, protect ourselves from that world by remaining in a sort of Christian bubble, filling our lives with church-centred activity, continually reassuring ourselves of the impregnability of our faith, but that will not be mission.

We can indeed make ourselves look very missionary by going all out to serve others or bring them to Christ, but if it is all done from within the bubble and for the sake of the bubble (and always to be talking about Jesus can be an excellent way of insulating ourselves, as well as driving those around us to drink), it is not true mission. Mission means going right out from 'the physical and spiritual upper room', into the world where no holds are barred. What then is meant by 'Eucharistic life'? It doesn't mean going to church every five minutes and it doesn't mean walling oneself in with Christian thoughts and Christian friends important though these are. Rather it means reproducing in everyday life the pattern of the Eucharist which is the pattern of Christ; living a life in which penitence and forgiveness are integral; open to the glory of God in even the most unexpected settings; listening for his Word in whatever is said and in the space between; testing one's belief against the belief and the unbelief of the world; offering oneself for others, and others to God, entering into the darkness, brokenness and bloodiness of things in the nakedness of unprotected faith and enjoying to the full our community with people of every possible kind and with the whole created order. We pray God to make us a living sacrifice, but by itself that's too narrow and negative; we must become in fact a living sacrament, giving with love and receiving with thanks.

◆ ***A Call to Birds of a Feather*** by Virginia Thesiger

> We could stay in the house of the Lord for ever,
> saying our prayers and singing His praises
> with people who think as we think coming
> to join in the comfort and peace of it all;
> to exchange the good news, to glow together
> friends among friends, birds of a feather.
>
> But there on the doorstep lies the world,
> turbulent, violent, sick and sorry,
> full of fierce arguments, weeping and loveless

(nothing like us who are blissful and beaming
singing our hymns in the house of the Lord).

Come let us open the door and step out
fearlessly into the dreadful confusion
of those who believe what we do not believe
of those who are seeking and those who are faithless
and those who seem lost to all love for their sins . . .

Out, out and let us radiantly run
to the stranger, the outcast, the sick unto death,
with our message of healing, our glorious hope,
our truth that turns hate into love,
grief into joy, rain into roses,
ill into well, dross into gold . . .
sharing the fruits that have fed us so often,
here as we sit in the house of the Lord
glowingly saying our prayers together,
friends among satisfied friends,
birds of an unruffled feather.

◆ *From* **The Gates of Heaven: The New Union Prayer Book**, by the General Conference of American Rabbis 5735

DOUBTS

Cherish your doubts for doubt is the handmaiden of truth.

Doubt is the key to the door of knowledge; it is the servant of discovery.

A belief which may not be questioned binds us to error, for there is incompleteness and imperfection in every belief.

Doubt is the touchstone of truth, it is the acid which eats away the false.

Let none fear for the truth; that doubt may consume it; for doubt is a testing of belief.

For truth, if it be truth, arises from each testing stronger, more secure. Those who would silence doubt are filled with fear; the house of their spirit is built on shifting sands.

But they that fear not doubt, and know its use, are founded on a rock.

They shall walk in the light of growing knowledge; the work of their hands shall endure.

Therefore let us not fear doubt but let us rejoice in its help: it is to the wise as a staff to the blind; doubt is the handmaiden of truth.

◆ *From* **Jacob's Ladder** by Michael Stancliffe

Michael Stancliffe wrote about the true way of remembering the past: 'Not as a looking back, but as a recalling'. Not, he said, 'as a leaving of the present in order to return to the past, but as a bringing back of the past into the present in such a way that what the world regards as dead and gone is alive and with us and having a quickening and practical effect upon our thinking here and now, today and tomorrow . . .' And that is a way of looking at things which can have important, healthy and most liberating consequences for ourselves. For once we have committed ourselves to this idea of our life as an inevitably on-going natural movement (and everything in the Bible, both Old Testament and New, supports that idea) and *that* movement a *dance*, that is, a movement with a pattern in it, then a great many things which bewilder and confuse us, or dismay, distract and sadden us will do so no longer. Once we accept that whether we like it or not, we are caught up in an on-going dance, then we see that it is senseless to make ourselves miserable by grieving over the past, that things are not what they were. We cannot go back, we cannot even stand still; and only those of us who are dead in heart can drop out. This is so very obvious – yet how many of us refuse to accept the plain fact. Edwin Muir was one of those who saw this clearly enough and expressed it in his short dialogue poem, 'The Way'.

◆ ***The Way*** by Edwin Muir

Friend I have lost the way
The way leads on
Is there another way?
The way is one.
I must retrace the track
It's lost and gone
Back I must travel back

None goes there none.
Then I'll make here my place
(the road leads on)
Stand still and set my face.
(the road leaps on)
Stay here forever stay
None stays here none.
I cannot find the way.
The way leads on.
Oh places I have passed
That journey's done
And what will come at last
The road leads on.

◆ *From* **The Centuries** by Thomas Traherne

THANKSGIVING

What diamonds are equal to my eyes;
what labyrinths to my ears;
what gates of ivory, or ruby leaves
to the double portals of my lips and teeth?
Is not sight a jewel?
Is not hearing a treasure?
Is not speech a glory?
O my Lord pardon my ingratitude,
and pity my dullness
who am not sensible of these gifts.
The freedom of thy beauty hath deceived me,
These things were too near to be considered.
Thou presentedst me with thy blessings
and I was not aware.

◆ *From* **Prayer of the Order of St Michael and St George**

Grant unto us, O Lord, the royalty of inward happiness and the serenity which comes from living close to Thee.

Daily renew in us the sense of joy and let Thy Eternal Spirit dwell in our souls and bodies, filling every corner of our hearts with light and gladness.

So that bearing about with us the infection of a good courage we may be diffusers of life, giving Thee thanks always for all things. Through Jesus Christ our Lord.

### ◆ *September 5th 1991*

*I have just been privileged to take part in a miracle: the opening of Global Co-operation House – International Centre for the Brahma Kumari World Spiritual University. The World Centre for Global Co-operation for a better world.*

*The miracle takes the shape of a beautiful building remarkable for its simplicity, its insights and above all for its atmosphere of peace and tranquillity.*

*Four million pounds were donated by people who believe in world co-operation to make their world a better place for all mankind.*

*A tree was planted on a derelict site in Willesden in 1988, followed by the laying of the foundation stone. Representatives from four continents brought a symbolic artefact from each of their homelands, and these artefacts were buried at the exact centre of the building. Then came the 'topping up' ceremony, when the whole conception began to come to life, and finally the triumphant opening when the miracle could be seen in its entirety.*

*This account makes it all sound so simple and straightforward, but it is only the instigators of the project who know of all that has gone into those four years of intense activity, planning and inspiration; the faith needed to overcome the seemingly insurmountable problems.*

*The world owes a tremendous debt of gratitude to the Brahma Kumaris and their World Spiritual University. They have been the miracle workers from the initial inspiration to its culmination.*

*I have been privileged to join in their meditations over the years and here I must record my deepest gratitude to Sister Jayanti who has given me so much of her valuable time and taught me so much about meditation.*

*The headquarters of the Brahma Kumari community is at Mount Abu, Rajasthan, India and from there came the Mount Abu Declaration issued at the summit conference in 1989. E.B.*

*The Mount Abu Declaration, 1989*

*'As a global family we share the same unique planet and share the same hopes and aspirations for a just and humane world. Yet as we*

*approach the dawn of the next millennium, we are concerned that life on earth is threatened.*

*Our beautiful planet is faced with a crisis of unprecedented magnitude. In many cultures, the moral fabric of society is challenged by violence, crime, addiction, denial of human rights and human dignity, and the disintegration of family life.*

*At the same time, we, the people of the world, are yearning for peace and a better world for ourselves and our children. How is it that with all the human skill and talent that exists, with all the achievements in technology, there is still grinding poverty, massive arms expenditure and a grave deterioration in the environment?*

*There is so much to be done and so many willing hands and hearts to do it.*

*What is needed is the spirit of co-operation and goodwill, the attitude of love and respect towards each other, the practice of positive and creative thinking, the application of moral and spiritual values in daily life, as well as action based on a shared vision of a better world.*

*Now is the time to call on the will and the clear vision of the people.*

> *"A vision without a task is but a dream*
> *A task without a vision is a drudgery*
> *A vision with a task can change the world."*

*The voice of the people must be heard. This Declaration is an acknowledgement that it is the people who, by their active participation and co-operation, can change the world.'*

*For those who would like to explore further, the address of the new centre in London is: Global Co-operation House, 65 Pond Lane, London NW10 2HH.*

◆ ***Longfellow***

And he wandered away and away
    With Nature the dear old nurse
Who sang to him night and day
    The rhymes of the universe.

And whenever the way seemed long
    Or his heart began to fail

She would sing a more wonderful song
Or tell a more wonderful tale.

◆ ***Robert Runcie,** from* **The Sir Francis Younghusband Memorial Lecture**, May 28th 1986

CHRISTIANITY AND WORLD RELIGIONS

If we trust the life-giving power of the spirit within and among us, we can meet each other in openness and trust; we can learn to explore together the moments of revelation and the spiritual pleasures which our respective faiths have handed down to us – a spark of divine life and a vision of holiness whereby the lives of countless people in past and present are nourished, sustained, transformed and sanctified.

. . . We need both courage and humility to recognise this work of the spirit among us in other faiths. It takes courage to acknowledge religious diversity as a rich spiritual source, rather than a cause for competition and tension. And it takes humility and sincerity to concede that there is a certain incompleteness in each of our traditions.

However diverse in their development and message, they always remain in a process of becoming, so that there is always room for growth towards a fuller, richer version of the truth. We must also realise that ultimately all religions possess a provisional, interim character as ways and signs to help us in our pilgrimage to Ultimate Truth and Perfection.

◆ *From* **The Spiritual Nature of Man** by Alistair Hardy

The believer who has communicated with his God is not merely a man who sees new truths of which the unbeliever is ignorant; he is a new man who is *stronger.* He feels within him more force, either to endure the trials of existence or to conquer them.

It is as though he were raised above the miseries of the world, because he is raised above his condition as a mere man, he believes he is saved from evil, under whatever form he may conceive this evil.

The first article in every creed is the belief in salvation by faith.

*This poem by Elizabeth Barrett Browning always makes me think of the Song of Songs, that paean of love and praise.*

How shall I love Thee? Let me count the ways.
I love thee to the depth and breadth and height
My soul can reach, when feeling out of sight
For the ends of Being and ideal grace
I love thee to the level of every day's
Most quiet need, by sun and candle light
I love thee freely, as men strive for Right.
I love thee purely, as they turn from Praise.
I love thee with the passion put to use
In my old griefs, and with my childhood's faith.
I love thee with a love I seemed to lose
With my lost saints – I love thee with the breath,
Smiles, tears of all my life – and if God choose,
I shall but love thee better after death.

◆ ***Hymn for Terce***

The Earth is filled with the Spirit of God.
Creative, Powerful, Free.
Encounter as a Wind Unseen.
Sweep through our hearts and renew us in God.
Life-giving breath from on high.
Love's energy working Love.
Sing to His glory, fling wide His praise.
People redeemed and set free,
Caught in the shout of Heaven's Joy.

◆ *From* **The Way of Salvation** by William Law

There is but one salvation for all mankind and that is the Life of God in the soul. God has but one design or intent towards all mankind and that is to introduce or generate His own Life, Light and Spirit in them, that all may be as so many images, temples and habitations of the Holy Trinity. This is God's will to all Christians, Jews and Heathens.

They are all equally the desire of His heart; His light continually waits for the entrance into all of them; 'His wisdom crieth, she putteth forth her voice,' not here or there, but everywhere, in all the streets of all the parts of the world.

Now there is but one possible way for man to attain his salvation, or Life of God in the soul. There is not one for the Jew, another for the Christian and a third for the Heathen. No, God is one, human nature is one, salvation is one and the way to it is one and that is the desire, for the soul turned to God.

When that desire is alive and breaks forth in any creature under heaven, then the lost sheep is found and the shepherd hath it upon his shoulder.

◆ ***Mystic Bonds that Unite Faiths*** by John Cole, *from* **The Times**, Saturday September 21st 1985

What is the mystic bond that unites holy men and women of many faiths and in particular those of Hinduism, Judaism, Christianity and Islam?

When they meet they know that they have much in common in that part of their being which is most precious to them. However great their differences of theology and forms of worship may be, they share and know they share in a mystic experience which gives meaning to their lives and to the Universe.

What is that experience and what meaning does it give to life? The mystery in the souls of religious men of many faiths is an intense awareness of a presence abiding with and within themselves and the world. About 500 BC a Hindu wrote, 'My son, there is nothing in the world that is not God's, spirit is everywhere, on the right, on the left, above and below, behind, in front. What is the world but Spirit?' The Jewish psalmist's theme is the same, 'Whither shall I go from thy spirit or whither shall I go from thy presence? If I climb up into heaven thou art there, if I go down into hell thou art there also.' Among Christians blessed Johannes Ruysbroek tells us 'The first and highest unity of man is in God, for all creatures depend on this unity for their being, their life and their preservation and if they be separated from God they fall into nothingness and become naught.'

In Islam one of the Sufi mystics writes:

In the valley, in the mountain, only God I see.
Him I have seen beside me oft in tribulation
In favour and in fortune only God I saw. Baba Kuhi

Such men like Enoch walk with God and recognise each other when they meet for their intense awareness of God's abiding presence is the same. The spiritual experience gives meaning both to their existence as individuals and to the world in which they live, delivering them from many of the problems of our western culture which so often ignores the verities of the spirit by failing to transcend 'the measure of man's mind'. Modern man's tragic quest for his identity does not exist, for the mystics who know that they come from God, the source of all, that they continue to exist only by the indwelling of God and their destiny is to return to God. For such men that is enough, they seek no further, they have found 'the pearl of great price'.

Without the vision of all-pervading divinity, life as many have found it, is 'a tale told by an idiot, full of sound and fury, signifying nothing', but to those granted the gift of God's presence in all things, 'Heaven and earth are full of his glory'.

◆ *From* **In Tune with the Infinite** by Ralph Waldo Trine

'There is only one religion. Whatever road I take joins the highway that leads to Thee', says the inspired writer in the Persian scriptures.

'Broad is the carpet that God has spread and beautiful are the colours he has given it.'

'The pure man respects every form of faith,' says the Buddhist. 'My doctrine makes no difference between high and low, rich and poor; like the sky, it has room for all and like the water, it washes all alike.' 'The broad-minded see the truth in different religions, the narrow-minded see only the difference,' says the Chinese. The Hindu has said 'The narrow-minded ask, "Is this man a stranger or is he of our tribe?" But to those in whom love dwells, the whole world is but one family.'

◆ *Letter* to **The Times**, *from* Peter Stokes, January 29th 1993

In times of uncertainty there will always be some who wait and look for faith, clearly defined, limited and expressed.

But there will always be others for whom the Christian faith is too great to be subjected to absolute definitions, however much we might wish it: it cannot be limited or put into pigeon-holes.

For while it is firmly rooted in history – it reaches back to Abraham and on from Jesus Christ – the Christian religion is spiritual or it is nothing; and the spirit, like the wind, cannot be tracked down or limited – 'It blows wherever it pleases' (John 3:8).

◆ *From* **The Cosmic Christ** by Ladislaus Boros

REDEMPTION IS UNIVERSAL

That anyone should be excluded from the salvation brought by Christ, that redemption should not be universal is something that young people especially just can't accept today. This is one of the most insistent questions; they often ask it with profound unease. Again and again they object to the tag 'Outside the Church there is no salvation', and its variations on it.

I have never ceased to be surprised by the scandal that this statement causes, because I have never found it to be purely negative or destructive, quite the opposite. One has only to apply one of the simplest rules of logic to the statement, 'There is no salvation outside the Church', and to express it in the reverse form, to obtain a different version with an entirely liberating effect: 'Wherever there is salvation, there is the Church'.

. . . Understood in that sense, this controversial doctrine is a positive assertion of freedom. What was scandalous becomes liberating. The Church is always present – in its effects and in what may be a concealed form – wherever people are sincerely trying to do what is good, fine and true; giving themselves totally to what is greater than themselves; serving their fellow men with utter dedication; and wholly committing themselves to a cause. Everywhere where this is happening, salvation is taking place. Everywhere where this is happening, the Church is.

◆ ***Hymn*** by F.W. Faber, *from* **The English Hymnal**, no. 499

There's a wideness in God's mercy
Like the wideness of the sea;
There's a kindness in his justice
Which is more than liberty.

There is no place where earth's sorrows
Are more felt than up in heaven;
There is no place where earth's failings
Have such kindly judgement given.

There is grace enough for thousands
Of new worlds as great as this;
There is room for fresh creations
In that upper home of bliss.

For the love of God is broader
Than the measures of man's mind;
And the heart of the Eternal
Is most wonderfully kind:

But we make his love too narrow
By false limits of our own;
And we magnify his strictness
With a zeal he will not own.

There is plentiful redemption
In the blood that has been shed;
There is joy in all the members
In the sorrows of the Head.

'Tis not all we owe to Jesus;
It is something more than all;
Greater good because of evil
Larger mercy through the fall.

If our love were but more simple,
We should take him at his word;

And our lives would be all sunshine
In the sweetnes of our Lord.

◆ *From* **The Kingdom of Edmund** by Priscilla Napier

*So now to many Englishmen it fell*
*To gather up the spiritual resources.*

By Andrewes, Herbert, and resounding Donne,
And Vaughan, who saw eternity's great ring
Of pure and endless light;
Jeremy Taylor, who beheld the world
No poisonous swamp of evil, from whose air
The godly must withdraw in holy flight,
But as a place where gratitude could brim
He could delight in all created things
Coming from God, and ministers to him.

Through grace of faith, and privilege of prayer
God was ubiquitous as sea, earth and air,
And we enclosed within Him; and our life
Through power of Him who came to us, could be
Thus ordered and thus fair.

They taught men that religion without goodness
Is but a superstition,
So also are those prayers
Nagging at God to give us special treatment;
As in a nervous flutter
Buying protection both in cash and kind.
Take heart – so ran their spiritual tuition –
In self-forgetfulness win peace of mind.
Fear God and keep his laws, and do not mutter.
Your praise and thanks you should most chiefly
utter.
Take heart, after your tears
There's laughter to be had, beyond the fears.

Fear God and keep his laws, the Christian way
Is not a murmur of this or the other creed
In the belief that this is all we need.
It is a road of life, and to be followed
With the whole being, all of every day.

Let us now praise famous men
And our fathers that begat us
Edmund among the rest;
The men who rode the storm
Learning the strength to follow
And hold the truth that matters
To leave the false and hollow
And not to fear reform.

Thank God for all who helped us
The great, the least, the best: Sorrow and joy must
    teach
And prayer and contemplation
The faith that these possessed;
That we at length may reach
Their land long since discovered
Beatitude unguessed
The Islands of the Blest.

◆ ***Hymnus Amoris*** by Axel Olrik

CHILDHOOD
Love gives me life
It clothes me as I grow up
It bathes me every day with joy.

YOUTH
Love is my hope and my desire
It shines for me like a star
I seek its fullness always.

MANHOOD
Love is my spring of water
Goodness flowers upon its banks
Love is my strength.

LOSS
Love is my grief
Nothing wounded me more deeply
Yet nothing is more dear.

OLD AGE
Love is my peace
And the glow of sunset
It pours its beauty on me that I may
give it back.
Love is my peace.

ANGELS
Source of light for the lowly
Lightning in a darkened land
Beacon broken in a thousand rays.
Torch of sacred wonders.

◆ ***Poem*** by Dorothy Law Holte

A LIFE IN YOUR HANDS

If a child lives with criticism
He learns to condemn,
If a child lives with hostility
He learns to fight,
If a child lives with ridicule
He learns to be shy,
If a child lives with shame
He learns to feel guilty,
If a child lives with tolerance
He learns to be patient,
If a child lives with encouragement
He learns confidence,

If a child lives with praise
He learns to appreciate,
If a child lives with fairness
He learns justice,
If a child lives with security
He learns to have faith,
If a child lives with approval
He learns to like himself,
If a child lives with acceptance and friendship
He learns to find love in the world.

◆ 4 ◆

# Moments of Vision

◆ *From* **Moments of Vision** by Kenneth Clark

How are the central obsessive images of the great artist related to the moments of vision which we all share? The question leads us to consider what has perhaps been too long deferred, the visionary powers of childhood. The child, the ordinary man, and the creative artist are all moved by a flash of self-identification in the same way, but there is no doubt that the child is moved more often and that these flashes illuminate his whole being with a more penetrating light. It was this fact that led Wordsworth to evolve what I suppose we must call his mystique of childhood. 'Thou best Philosopher, thou Eye among the blind . . . Mighty Prophet, Seer blest.' It goes rather far, as a poet should. Still we must admit that the heightened perceptions of children are within the experience of us all; and we can hardly help agreeing with Wordsworth when he says that they

> . . . surely must belong
> To those first-born affinities that fit
> Our new existence to existing things.

There is really no rational explanation why certain natural objects – flowers, springs and streams, clouds, bird's nests, trees – seemed so magical to us in our infancy; or why we still attach so much value to them when they are seen afresh for us by poets and artists. Now though theories of a collective unconscious come dangerously close to crystal-gazing and the planchette, there is a quantity of evidence for believing that man has always instinctively needed certain images to nourish his spirit, just as he needs certain foods to nourish his body. . . . The moment of vision, although it is a fresh individual experience for all of us, gains its power because it is a morsel of collective experience as well. The poet and artist born, as we all are, with a capacity for delighted self-discovery in certain symbols, finds amongst them a few which outlive his childhood because they nourish the centre of his creative being. So Ruskin discovered his responsiveness to sparkle and filigree, to fireflies and twig tracery; and Coleridge surrendered himself to the pale translucency of the moon. So Leonardo secreted memories of the mountain streams at Vinci, of 'the lizards and other strange small creatures which haunt an Italian vineyard' and so Dürer was obsessed by the hands which had chiselled gigantically above and around his infant head; indeed it is questionable if there is any central image in an artist's work which did not come to him as a moment of vision in childhood, and even the poet whose references to things seen are inevitably more incidental – the seasoning rather than the substance of his work – constantly draws his images from a single type of visual experience. These flashes which seemed at first to be no more than short – though mysteriously important – accidents in a work of art, turn out to be like sparks shot up from the molten centre of the imagination.

◆ ***Sir Henry Newbolt***

Lord, tho' I lived on earth, the child of earth, yet was I fathered by the starry sky. Give me to drink of the sweet spring that leaps from Memory's fount, wherein no cypress sleeps.

There shalt thou drink, O Soul, and therein slake the immortal longing of thy mortal thirst; so of thy Father's life shalt thou partake, and be forever that which thou wert at first.

◆ *From* **A Wound Deep in the Heart** by Jean Vanier

Our heart is made for the limitless, the infinite. We yearn for more than the finite. Yet all that we see around us is limited, finite. There is a deep dissatisfaction within us, urging us forward and impelling us to flee reality.

Each one of us is called to welcome this wound in the hope of discovering within our deepest heart, the heart of a child. We are allowed to be children and to enter into the world of the child: a world of trust, tenderness, simplicity and wonder. The child is an uncomplicated, unified being, a creature of tenderness. Trust is an extraordinary quality which unifies the child. This trust, tenderness and simplicity bring the child into a place of wonderment.

Wonder is close to thanksgiving, to gratitude and to contemplation. It is the acknowledgement that we are not masters but children, and that the universe is our dwelling place, our home. These child-like qualities spring from the wounded and the awareness that God is our Father and thus we are safe.

We are called to grow with this heart of a child, and to take part in the struggle to make this world a place where we human beings can live and be together simply, as children.

◆ ***Reconciliation*** by George Russell (1867–1935)

I begin through the grass once again to be bound to the Lord.
  I can see through a face that is faded, the face full of rest.
Of the earth, of the mother, my heart with her heart in accord.
As I lie 'mid the cool green tresses that mantle her breast
  I begin once again through the grass to be bound to the Lord.

By the hand of a child I am led to the throne of the King,
  For a touch that now fevers me not is forgotten and far,
And his infinite sceptred hands that sway us can bring
Me in dreams from the laugh of a child to the song of a star.
  On the laugh of a child I am borne to the joy of the King.

◆ *From* **The Excursion** by William Wordsworth

I have seen
A curious child, who dwelt upon a tract
Of inland ground, applying to his ear
The convolutions of a smooth-lipped shell
To which in silence hushed, his very soul
Listened intensely; and his countenance soon
Brightened with joy; for from within were heard
Murmurings, whereby the monitor expressed
Mysterious union with its native sea.
Even such a shell the universe itself

Is to the ear of Faith; and there are times
I doubt not, when to you it doth impart
Authentic tidings of invisible things:
Of ebb and flow, and ever-during power;
And central peace, substituting at the heart
Of endless agitation.

◆ *From* **Reading with the Heart** by Richard J. Foster. He writes on the Sacrament of the present moment by de Caussade.

'In his letters, de Caussade himself provides counsel in how to read, counsel that applies equally well to the reading of his own work.

'Read quietly, slowly, word for word to enter into the subject more with the heart than the mind . . . From time to time make short pauses to allow these truths time to flow through all the recesses of the soul and to give occasion for the operation of the Holy Spirit who, during these powerful pauses and times of silent attention engraves and imprints these heavenly truths in the heart . . . Should this peace and rest last for a longer time it will be all the better. When you find that your mind wanders resume your reading and continue thus, frequently renewing these same pauses.

'Finally, I would suggest that as you read you do not look for a precise logical development of themes. Rather look for the perceptive insight into human life, look for the winsome combination of wisdom and devotion, look for the sudden burst of joy.'

◆ ***A Prayer for Enlightenment***, source unknown

O, Thou who art the source and ground of all truth,
The Light of Lights who hast opened the minds of men to discern the
things that are, guide me today I beseech Thee in my reading.
Give me grace to choose the right books and to read them in the right way.
Give me wisdom to abstain as well as to persevere.
Let the Bible have its proper place: and grant that as I read I may be alive to the stirrings of the Holy Spirit in my soul.

*I owe a great debt of gratitude to Ted Hughes for introducing me to a fascinating book called* On Common Ground *which has opened many windows for me. It is written by Miss Jill Pirrie and includes poetry written for the W.H. Smith competition for schoolchildren's poems.*

*Many of these leave one amazed by their perception and their vast vocabulary. I believe that 25 per cent of the prize winners came from Miss Pirrie's school at Halesworth in Suffolk.*

*I feel that Ted Hughes' poem 'The Thought Fox' must have given the idea to some of the thought poems written by the children. E.B.*

◆ *From* **Selected Poems (1957–1981**) by Ted Hughes

THE THOUGHT FOX

I imagine in this midnight's forest
Something else is alive
Beside the clock's loneliness.

Through the window I see no star
Something more near
Though deeper within darkness
Is entering the loneliness.

Cold, delicately as the dark snow
A fox's nose touches twig, and leaf,
Two eyes serve a movement, that now
And again now, and now, and now.

Sets neat prints into the snow
Between trees, and warily a lame
Shadow lags by stump and in hollow
Of a body that is bold to come.

Across clearings, an eye,
A widening deepening greenness
Brilliantly, concentratedly,
Coming about its own business.

Till with a sudden sharp hot stink of fox
It enters the dark hole of the head
The window is starless still, the clock ticks
The page is printed.

◆ ***Winter*** by David Basset, aged nine years seven months. This was written as a prose paragraph suitable for turning into blank verse.

'Winter is cold, winter is desertless, nothing, a huge sparkling whiteness. A huge world of its own. A bleak wind, a cold world.

'No creature dares show its face, all animals use the instinct of their kind and hide away under stones and boulders, or have made a mossy bed to last winter's desertless nothing.'

◆ *From* **Collected Poems** by Edwin Muir

CHILDHOOD

Long time he lay upon the sunny hill,
    To his father's house below securely bound.
Far off the silent, changing sound was still,
    With the black islands thick around.

He saw each separate height, each vaguer hue,
    where the massed islands rolled in mist away,
And though all ran together in his view
    He knew that unseen straits between them lay.

Over the sound a ship so slow would pass
    That in the black hill's gloom it seemed to lie.
The evening sound was smooth like sunken glass,
    And time seemed finished ere the ship had passed by.

Grey tiny rocks slept round him where he lay,
    Moveless as they, more still as evening came,
The grasses threw straight shadows far away
    And from the house his mother called his name.

◆ *From* **Profitable Wonders: Aspects of Thomas Traherne** by Julia Smith

'Traherne looks at the world with the eye of a poet and he is with Henry Vaughan among the small number (stretching from Dante through Wordsworth to Edwin Muir) who exalt the holiness of the child's perception: exalt it, and at moments retrieve it. Most people retrieve this way of seeing only when they fall in love, like Tolstoy's Levin in *Anna Karenina*.

'What he then saw he never saw again. Two children going to school, some pigeons which flew down from a roof, and a few loaves put outside a baker's window. All these things were so unusually beautiful that Levin laughed and cried with joy.'

In this context I am reminded of a remarkable Romanes lecture by Kenneth Clark entitled 'Moments of Vision', a phrase he applies not to prophetic writings, 'whose authors have usually felt that things which a man can see with his own eyes were not sufficiently awe-inspiring to be communications of the divine', but to those 'flashes' when familiar objects are seen in the light of eternity.

And these experiences, which we all had in childhood (whether we can recall them or not), he relates to a collective memory. He quotes this illuminating passage from Coleridge:

'In looking at objects of nature . . . as at yonder moon dim glimmering through the dewy window-pane, I seem rather to be seeking a symbolic language for something within me that forever and already exists than observing anything new. Even when this latter is the case, yet still I have always an obscure feeling, as if that new phenomenon were a dim awakening of a forgotten or hidden truth of my inner nature.'

◆ *From* **Exploration into Love**

God are you there?
like an opening bud unaware
awareness awakes unafraid
in a trust wholly given
God's love flows out into his world
through the heart of a child.

◆ *From* **A Dusty Mirror: Thoughts and Poems** by Susan Wood

FREEDOM

I do not possess it
Must win it
Every day,
Yet it is the one gift
I can give you.
'Twould seem to be
Love's opposite,
And yet because
Of love I give it –
Freedom.

◆ *From* **The Tao of Pooh** by Benjamin Hoff

In the story of the Ugly Duckling, when did the Ugly Duckling stop feeling ugly? When he realised that he was a Swan. Each of us has something Special, a Swan of some sort, hidden inside somewhere. But until we recognise that it's there, what can we do but splash around, treading water? The Wise are Who they Are. They work with what they've got and do what they can do.

There are things about ourselves that we need to get rid of, there are things we need to change. But at the same time, we do not need to be too desperate, too ruthless, too combative. Along the way to usefulness and happiness, many of those things will change themselves, and the others can be worked on as we go. The first thing we need to do is recognise and trust our own Inner Nature, and not lose sight of it. For within the Ugly Duckling is the Swan, inside the Bouncy Tigger is the Rescuer who knows the Way, and in each of us is something Special, and that we need to keep.

For a long time they looked at the river beneath them, saying nothing, and the river said nothing too, for it felt very quiet and peaceful on that summer afternoon.

'Tigger is all right really,' said Piglet lazily. 'Of course he is,' said Christopher Robin. 'Everybody is really.' 'That's what I think,' said Pooh. 'But I don't suppose I'm right.' 'Of course you are,' said Christopher Robin.

◆ *A Father's Prayer* by General Douglas MacArthur

Build me a son, O Lord, who will be strong enough to know when he is weak, and brave enough to fall himself when he is afraid: one who will be proud and unbending in honest defeat, and humble and gentle in victory.

Build me a son whose wishbone will not be where his backbone should be, a son who will know thee – and that to know himself is the foundation of knowledge.

Lead him, I pray, not in the path of ease and comfort, but under the stress and spur of difficulties and challenge. Here let him learn to stand up in the storm; here let him learn compassion for those who fall.

Build me a son whose heart will be clear, whose goal will be high; a son who will master himself before he seeks to master other men; one who will learn to laugh, yet never forget how to weep; one who will reach into the future, yet never forget the past.

And after all these things are his, add, I pray, enough of a sense of humour, so that he may always be serious, yet never take himself seriously. Give him humility, so that he may always remember the simplicity of true greatness, the open mind of true wisdom, the weakness of true strength.

Then I, as his father, will dare to whisper, 'I have not lived in vain'.

◆ *From* **David Cecil: A Portrait by his Friends**, collected and introduced by Hannah Cranborne

BY GERALD IRVINE

*An address given by Lord David Cecil at St James' Piccadilly in 1978 on the value of literature.*

We are divided, we are born with a soul that derives from a spiritual region and partakes of its nature, which is a desire for perfection. But we are born into a fallen world, a sinful world, which is imperfect, limited, flawed, disappointing. The result is that the soul isn't at home, not really at home, in this world. Now what art does is to give us an image of perfection which softens the soul's longing, it gives a glimpse of the world unfallen and by so doing, it nourishes and strengthens and inspires us. Great art draws its power from what is the first Source of spiritual life, the first and final Source. And it reveals a profounder reality than we see in this world, that is apparent on this imperfect earth. Shakespeare's vision – it isn't only more beautiful than we see, it's truer, deeper and the perfection it shows is not a dream, a day-dream or a delusion, it is something that lives more intensely than anything in the transient world we know.

◆ *From* **Full Circle** by Dame Janet Baker

Ultimately, 'religion' means one simple thing; it is the relationship an individual has with his Maker. It is a one-to-one affair. I have come to the conclusion that at all the crisis times, one is utterly alone. When I am singing, regardless of those who taught me, those who have worked with me on a piece of music, regardless of the musicians surrounding me, I am absolutely alone. There is no one to get me through the final moment of opening my mouth and doing it except myself and One Other; at times of great distress or bereavement, I have felt exactly the same, alone, but alone with God. There is no security in the world or in people, however much we love them. No one can actually see inside another's heart and mind; we all presume and sometimes quite successfully, that we can share each other's joys and sorrows; in a certain way we do. But the miracle of belief is that the inevitable alone-ness reveals Someone else. That Someone else is, if you like, 'inside us', closer than that. He knows everything about us, everything we say and do and are. And knowing all this, loves us without reservation.

◆ ***Dorothea Eastwood, 1947***

Once as I lay thinking of God's love and wishing that I might feel it more strongly and surely, it struck me very forcibly that I had never yet asked that I should . . . and even as I thought this I seemed to understand something of his love for all men, seeing it as warm beams of light that glowed alike for sinners and the pure in heart. And because to the pure in heart all things are pure, so to these the beams were not darkened nor deflected, for the saints burned with their own radiance and their light mingled with the light of God and the two united together clear and brilliant.

Yet there are not many who received the light in its first purity, for most moved in a dark mist which they shed about them as the pure shed their glow. Upon this darkness the beam of God's love beat ceaselessly; they fell with the same force, warmth and brilliance as upon the saint, but because of the sinner's own darkness they could not penetrate and illumine him. Instead they encircled him so that he sat within the little black or grey cocoon of his own spinning, unaware of the glory by which he was encompassed. And I saw too, that by my own love for a fellow creature I could assist God's love to penetrate this darkness. His love is infinitely, immeasurably greater than mine, yet my narrow beam might act as a needle-point to prick the way for this vast radiance to enter. I saw that it was even more vital to love the sinner than the saint, for the saint was already himself the light of God's love, but without human love, the sinner's darkness grew denser and spread further.

And suddenly I saw that I, a sinner too, was surrounded by this power and this glory. I had to look and to know what I needed and the light came rushing in. If I would ask, I too would receive it in all its purity and if I received it there was nothing I could not do.

But I had grown used to my dark mist; and I was afraid the light might blind me, afraid I might be lost in its vastness; I saw that like all the other roads to truth and beauty, it required not only the sudden vision of arrival but much trudging on the long journey and much study of maps and help from fellow travellers. Patience too and strength and an inextinguishable hope and faith. And yet this love of God's was the source of all those things.

◆ *From* **David Cecil: A Portrait by his Friends**, collected and introduced by Hannah Cranborne

BY ISAIAH BERLIN

His lecture on Walter Pater in 1985 is an exquisite appreciation of the aesthetic approach to life, which meant a very great deal to him, and which he defended in an unfavourable climate, as emerged in his inaugural Lecture.

Against the current stream of the times, in 1949 and again in 1957, he declared that the central purpose of art was to give delight, not to instruct, nor to disturb, nor to explain, nor to praise or condemn a movement or idea, a regime, nor to help build a better world in the service of a church, a party, a nation, a class, but to irradiate the soul with a light which God had granted the artist the power to shed, and the reader or listener to understand, delight in, and thereby be drawn nearer the divine Creator.

◆ ***Sir Yehudi Menuhin***: His dictum on musical perfection

The most blessed and privileged of all callings is that of the musician who acts as an interpreter, healer, consoler, and above all as humble servant.

These are the human rules I would endeavour to cultivate among my beloved group of young students, who enrich my school not only with their burgeoning talents but with the great diversity of their backgrounds.

◆ ***Dame Janet Baker*** *from* The Eric Symes Abbott Memorial Lecture, 1988

Dame Janet speaks of the questions put to her by journalists:

Two things crop up with regularity.

'Are you religious? Are musicians religious?'

Both of these questions are too enormous to be discussed with a journalist and I usually refuse to be drawn on either.

Tonight is a marvellous opportunity since we are remembering a man whose vocation was communication through the priesthood and it is in just these terms that I feel able to reply.

Yes, I do feel music is a religious calling and I do feel artists are called to a very special priesthood in the sense that we minister to those who need us. Particularly as performers, we are the mediators.

The priest mediates between God and his people.

I believe every artist is in some sense involved in the priesthood even if perhaps unconsciously. We serve something greater than ourselves: one is made very much aware of this every time one re-creates a work of a great composer. At the inner core of music is the possibility that performing can touch and change the human heart. This is not an attribute over which musicians have the slightest control.

We know that it is there, we know that sometimes it appears. We know that when it does, we, the performers, are as much in its power as the audience is and I believe that a power which can touch and change can only be divine.

## ◆ *II Corinthians 4:17–18*

For our light affliction which is but for a moment, worketh for us a far more exceeding and eternal weight of glory.

While we look not at the things which are seen, but at the things which are not seen, for the things which are seen are temporal but the things which are not seen are eternal.

## ◆ *From* **In Tune with the Infinite** by Ralph Waldo Trine

Everything exists in the unseen before it is manifested or realised in the seen and in this sense it is true that the unseen things are the real, while the things that are seen are the unreal. The unseen things are *cause* – the seen are *effect*. The unseen things are the eternal, the seen things are the changing, the transient.

## ◆ *From* **Poetry in the Making** by Ted Hughes

### WORDS AND EXPERIENCES

Many people, perhaps most of us, think in words all the time, and keep a perpetual running commentary going or a mental conversation, about everything that comes under our attention or about something in the back of our minds. But it is not essential. And the people who think in dumb pictures and dim sensings seem to manage just as well. Maybe they manage even better. You can imagine who is likely to be getting most out of reading the gospels, for instance: the one who discusses every sentence word by word and argues the contradictions and questions every obscurity and challenges every absurdity, or the one who imagines, if only for a few seconds, but with the shock of full reality, just what it must have been like to be standing near when the woman touched Christ's garment and he turned round.

It is the same with all our experiences of life: the actual substance of it, the material facts of it, embed themselves in us quite a long way from the world of words. It is when we set out to find words for some seemingly quite simple experience that we begin to realise what a huge gap there is between our understanding of what happens around us and inside us, and the words we have at our command to say something about it.

. . . Because it is occasionally possible, just for a brief moment, to find the words that will unlock the doors of all those many mansions inside the head and express something – perhaps not much, just something – of the crush of information that presses in on us from the way a crow flies over and the way a man walks and the look of a street and from what we did one day a dozen years ago.

Words that will express something of the deep complexity that makes us precisely the way we are, from the momentary effect of the barometer to the force that created men distinct from trees.

Something of the inaudible music that moves us along in our bodies from moment to moment like water in a river. Something of the spirit of the snowflake in the water of the river. Something of the duplicity and the relativity and the merely fleeting quality of all this. Something of the almighty importance of it and something of the utter meaninglessness. And when words can manage something of this, and manage it in a moment of time, and in that same moment make out of it all the vital signature of a human being – not of an atom, or of a geometrical diagram, or a heap of lenses – but of a human being, we call it poetry.

◆ *From* **The Eye of the Eagle** by David Adam

One of the great moments of our life is when we suddenly have our eyes opened, and it is as if we see for the first time.

We say with the blind man from St John's Gospel, 'I once was blind but now I see'. Often we do not know how this sight or insight came about, but we do know that our vision has been extended. A prayer by Origen that I like using begins with the words, 'May the Lord Jesus touch our eyes as He did those of the blind man'. Then we shall see in the visible things those things which are invisible.

That is something which the Celtic Church seemed to do a lot more easily than we do today – 'to see in the visible things those things which are invisible'. I do not believe that they saw God in all His glory any more than we do, but they certainly saw signs of His Presence. They were aware of creation pointing towards its Creator and because creation has a Creator we are offered a relationship through it to Him.

. . . They saw a universe ablaze with His glory, suffused with a Presence that calls, nods and beckons, a creation personally united with its Creator in every atom and fibre. There was nothing in this creation that need be without, or was without, that glory.

Through all things there was a chance of a personal relationship with God.

◆ *From* **God As Spirit** by G.W.H. Lampe

SPIRIT OF GOD AND SPIRIT OF MAN

A passage in Keith Ward's book *The Concept of God*, runs as follows:

At the centre of the human self there is some form of union or encounter with a reality which is felt to be both beyond the individual self and yet somehow at the very root of one's personal being . . . One may find within oneself a sustaining power which is beyond one's individual consciousness and yet at the centre of one's being, and which contains inspirational and creative resources upon which the conscious self can draw.

The twofold concept of spirit, divine and human, can serve excellently to give clear theological expression to this experience of a reality which transcends the human self and is yet immanent at the centre and root of its being. Indeed it points us further, to the truth that all personal communion between transcendent God and man involves God's immanence within man – nothing less, in fact, than an incarnation of God as Spirit in every man as a human spirit.

◆ ***The Vine*** by Dorothea Eastwood

MOMENTS OF VISION

[*To R.B.B. and D.C.B.*]

I saw with dreamer's eyes the other night
A Vine with leaves made all of throbbing light
That climbed the starred and deep blue wall of heaven
And curled and wound its fingers through the Seven.
Its leaves of crystal and its golden grapes
Were like the stars and full moon in their shapes,
And round that fruit and each still, crystal leaf
Burned the light's flame to keep away a thief.

And as I gazed in wonder in my dreams,
Out of the boughs there flowed bright, singing streams
It seemed I saw and heard this magic Vine
Pour music out like an enchanted wine,
Music more lovely than the sound of seas
Or reeds that kiss the night's slow-wandering breeze
Or birds that in their morning joy must fling
Songs to the sky because the Sun takes wings.

I asked within myself, 'What ecstasy
Can so inspire to music even this tree?'
And then I saw HIM coming down the hill,
The hill of Night – and all the stars stood still,
And all the glorious branches as He came
Pulsed with melody that leaped like flame,
And all the world was filled with praise and awe –
And this, a child in dreams I saw! I saw!

Yet not believing one so great as He
Would notice a small nightgowned thing like me
I stole where I could watch Him pause and stand
To part the fiery leaves with unburned hand.
I thought I hid in a deep well of shade,
But as He lifted back and gently laid
Those leaves aside to show the fruit's own light,
I knew He saw me yet I felt no fright.

Only I had such longing to once eat
And taste the golden grapes, moon-round and sweet
That now I dared disturb Him at His task
And boldly left the gloom that I might ask:
And yet before the words had faltered out
He knew my longing, and turning about,
Smiled, and as the music died to a low lute,
'You ask for much,' He said, 'to ask this fruit.

'Know, child, that for these boughs my blood was shed,
That they might live I lay among the dead;
To sweeten the wild juices of this vine,
I drank in agony a bitter wine.
Yet take and eat in memory of me
The grapes of light from my heavenly tree:
Then at Earth's dawn, when we two seem to part,
Plant the gold seeds in thy small earthly heart.'

And so I eat and still in dreams I see
That vine of joy, the shining heavenly tree.
I bear the seed, I hear the singing boughs
That glow with radiance as a clear wine glows:
And through the flying dream that sleeping men
Speak of as day, I long for dusk again –
For there, in dreams of truth I find the light,
And see His splendour on the hill of Night.

◆ 5 ◆

# The Language of Silence

# MEDITATION

## LIVING OUR PRAYER AND PRAYING OUR LIVES

*There are so many ways of praying. I think it was Evelyn Underhill who said, 'Pray as you can and not as you can't'. One can only speak from one's own experience and for me Father John Main's method of meditation with the mantra, to which I have only lately been introduced, seems for me like coming home after a long journey. For those who haven't experienced this way of praying, it is a very ancient way of Christian meditation, dating from pre-apostolic times.*

*John Cassian and the Desert Fathers followed this way, using for their mantras an Aramaic word,* Ma-ra-na-tha, *which translated means 'Come Lord Jesus'. This way of praying seems to me to avoid the anxieties we all must have of seeming to inform the Almighty of what He already knows, of telling Him what He should be doing about it, and of asking Him for things He has already given and continues to give.*

*I think what has charmed me most about John Main's teaching is his insistence that it is the Holy Spirit of God praying in and through us if only we can be silent, still and open. As St Paul has said, 'We do not know how to pray but the Holy Spirit prays in us with sighs too deep for words.'*

*I have included several quotations from John Main's books and tapes, but there are so many more which can be obtained from The Christian Meditation Centre, 29 Campden Hill Road, London W8. The tapes of Father Laurence Freeman, his successor, are also obtainable and are enormously helpful and informative. E.B.*

◆ *From* **Moment of Christ** by John Main

It is our conviction that the central message of the New Testament is that there is really only one prayer and that this prayer is the prayer of Christ. It is a prayer that continues in our hearts day and night. I can describe it only as the stream of love that flows between Jesus and his Father. That stream of love is the Holy Spirit.

Again it is our conviction that it is the most important task for any human life that we should become as open as possible to this stream of love. We have to allow that prayer to become our prayer, we have to enter into the experience of being swept out of ourselves – beyond ourselves into the wonderful prayer of Jesus – this great cosmic river of love.

*In preparing my anthologies, retreats and led meditations, I have used the following prayer, slightly adapted, written by Bishop George Appleton in his great humility.*

*O Eternal Word, give me a word to touch the hearts*
*of those who trust and hope in you.*
*Don't let me cover it with too many words of my own.*
*Don't let me be afraid of what they will think of me.*
*Help me to choose and write so that it gives them*
*confidence that it comes from you to me as well as to them.*
*Amen.*

*The world is going through great tribulation at the present time and we feel so powerless to help, but I believe from the bottom of my heart, that 'Prayer is a means by which the love of God is released into the world'. It is surely only by the power of God's love working through us that men's hearts will be changed.*

*He has decreed that we should be a necessary part in the working out of His purpose, and prayer is one of the ways in which He can use us.*

*Pope Paul in one of his talks reminds us of God's gift to us of His Holy Spirit to be with us always.*

*He said: 'God has given us His Holy Spirit. What more could God do for us? What more could God do for us than that?'*

*It is too wonderful for us to be able to realise fully, but I think the words in a Jewish prayer book express this best of all:*

*'There lives a God and his presence is the glow in the human heart.'*

*We have all experienced this glow at some special times in our lives, however fleetingly, but we are not always aware of the source from which it comes.*

*It has been said that it is not so much our ability that God wants of us, but our availability as we wait in loving silence, giving the Holy Spirit space to breathe in and through us.*

*Then perhaps He will show us what He wishes us to do, but if not we shall just go on loving and waiting till we find that inner peace which will stay with us through the storms and tragedies we meet in life.*

*I have heard it suggested that silent meditation is a selfish way of praying, that intercession and petition are a more outgoing and comprehensive form of prayer, but I think the following poem by Michel Quoist describes most vividly the total commitment to others which is included in the 'prayer of loving attention'.*

*The waiting upon God on behalf of a suffering world. E.B.*

◆ ***Prayer of Life*** by Michel Quoist

To be there before you, Lord, that's all
To shut the eyes of my body
To shut the eyes of my soul,
And be still and silent,
To expose myself to you who are there
  exposed to me
I am willing to feel nothing, Lord.
To see nothing,
To hear nothing
Empty of all images
In the darkness.
Here I am, simply
To meet you without obstacles
In the silence of faith.
Before you, Lord.
But, Lord, I am not alone
I can no longer be alone
I am a crowd, Lord,
For men live within me.
I have met them.
They have come in,
They have settled down
They have worried me.
They have tormented me

They have devoured me.
And I have allowed it, Lord, that they
might be nourished and refreshed.
I bring them to you in exposing myself
to you
Here I am,
Here they are,
Before you, Lord.

◆ ***Prayer*** from West Malling Abbey

Be silent
still
aware
for there in your own heart
the Spirit is at prayer
listen and learn
open and find
heart wisdom
CHRIST.

◆ *From* **Creative Silence** by Denis Duncan

In every area of life, one principle holds true. We cannot give out unless we take in.

Without the falling rain, the reservoirs go down. Without the gentle breeze, the windmill remains motionless. Without the gift of water, the rivers fail, the mountain streams dry up. Without the appropriate amount of food, strength diminishes. Without sleep, we do not have energy.

It is the same in the life of the spirit. Unless we receive the gift of grace, we have nothing to offer to others. Unless we drink at the well of running water, we cannot give the water of life to others. Unless we receive the love of Him who first loved us, we have no hope of finding the energy of love we are to offer to our neighbour, our brother, the world.

If, therefore, the giving out of love, of healing demands all the effort and energy I have suggested, there must come a time when love must rest and take in. Peace is love resting. It is love resting in order to be renewed. The renewal takes place in silence.

Let silence reign, so that the Spirit can come when we are silent within. In that creative inner silence, the miracle of grace is wrought.

◆ *From* **God of a Hundred Names**, collected and arranged by Barbara Greene and Victor Gollancz (translated by B.G.)

Lord, the Scripture says: 'There is a time for silence and a time for speech'. Saviour, teach me the silence of humility, the silence of vision, the silence of love, the silence of perfection, the silence that speaks without words, the silence of faith.

Lord, teach me to silence my own heart that I may listen to the gentle movement of the Holy Spirit within me and sense the depths which are of God.

◆ *From* **Inner Journey, Outer Journey** by James Roose-Evans

CREATIVE SILENCE

Once we have found our way into the deep inner silence, that form of prayer which is without words, it becomes like a seed planted within us – we have only to water it regularly, and it will send down deep roots, and grow into our own tree.

. . . Each one of us has a seed of life within us which must create the form or body that will be its inevitable fulfilment, like those multi-hued sea-shells, each one of which is unique, which the sea animal creates to house most perfectly its own particular spark of life. Each one of us has our own myth to live, our own song to sing, our own tale to tell and if we are to fulfil it we need the same courage that the professional artist requires. The spiritual process exactly mirrors the creative one.

◆ ***St Augustine***, Sermon 34

You sing, of course you sing, I can hear you
But make sure that your life sings the same tune
as your mouth.
Sing with your voices
Sing with your lips
Sing with your lives.
The singer himself is the song.

◆ ***Before Prayer***, source unknown

I weave a silence on my lips
I weave a silence into my mind
I weave a silence into my heart
I close my ears to distractions
I close my eyes to attractions
I close my heart to temptations.

Calm me O Lord as you stilled the storm
Still me O Lord keep me from harm
Let all the tumult within me cease
Enfold me Lord in your peace.

◆ ***A Self-Portrait of Indian Existence*** by Ohiyesa *from* **Touch the Earth**, compiled by T.C. McLuhan

The man who preserves his selfhood is ever calm and unshaken by the storms of existence – not a leaf, as it were astir on the tree; not a ripple upon the surface of the shining pool – his, in the mind of the unlettered sage, is the ideal attitude and conduct of life.

If you ask him: 'What is silence?' he will answer, 'It is the great Mystery, the holy silence is His voice.' If you ask, 'What are the fruits of silence?' he will say, 'They are self-control, true courage or endurance, patience, dignity and reverence. Silence is the cornerstone of character.'

◆ *From* **Christian Meditation** by John Main

Meditation is concerned not so much with thinking as with being. And in contemplative prayer we seek to become the person we are called to be, not by thinking about God but by being with Him.

Simply to be with Him is to be drawn into being the person He calls us to be.

This is the message of Jesus' injunction to seek the kingdom first and then all else will be given . . .

Our aim in Christian prayer is to allow God's mysterious and silent presence within us to become more and more, not only *a* reality, one of several to which we give what Cardinal Newman called 'notional assent', but *the* reality which gives meaning, shape and purpose to everything we do, to everything we are. And so prayer is not the time for words, however beautifully and sincerely phrased. All our words are wholly inadequate when we enter into mysterious communion with God whose Word is before and after all other words.

◆ ***Thou Art God***, source unknown

Thou art the peace of all things calm
Thou art the place to hide from harm
Thou art the light that shines in dark
Thou art the heart's eternal spark
Thou art the door that's open wide
Thou art the guest who waits inside
Thou art the stranger at the door
Thou art the calling of the poor
Thou art my Lord and with me still
Thou art my love, keep me from ill
Thou art the light, the truth, the way
Thou art my Saviour this very day.

◆ *From* **Collected Poems** by Rabindranath Tagore

I feel that all the stars shine in me
The world breaks into my life like a flood.
The flowers blossom in my body.
All the youthfulness of land and water smokes like an incense in my heart; and the breath of all things plays on my thoughts as on a flute.

◆ *From* **Women Mystics of the Twentieth Century** by Anne Bancroft

WEAVERS OF WISDOM

Kathleen Raine speaks of a world of ancient symbols, a world which many of us may not be aware of. She believes that each of us carries within ourself a certain sense of something known, a recollection of something we had forgotten, an assent, a coming into our own; anamnesis Plato called this awakening of knowledge we did not know ourselves to possess.

Such knowledge, she believes, is of a different level of reality from the one we live in and we hear whispers of its presence all our lives, coming to us in moments of insight as clarity and beauty, not a sterile beauty, but one which expresses all that is joyful, all that is clear.

◆ *From* **The Contemplative Life** by Thomas Merton

Behold my beloved.

I have shown you the power of silence, how thoroughly it heals and how fully pleasing it is to God.

Wherefore I have written to you to show yourselves strong in the work you have undertaken so that you may know that it is by silence that the saints grew, that it was because of silence that the power of God dwelt in them, because of silence that the mysteries of God were known to them.

◆ *From* **Weavers of Wisdom** by Anne Bancroft

WOMEN MYSTICS OF THE TWENTIETH CENTURY

Tylah Nitsch writes of the deep religious feelings of the native American Indians and of their way of perceiving existence.

The Senecas believe that during silent communication, the physical body underwent stages of healing and upliftment.

The feeling of well-being and self-understanding became the reward for Entering into the Silence. Being at peace with oneself and in harmony with the surroundings fortified each succeeding experience.

I listen and hear the silence
I listen and see the silence
I listen and taste the silence
I listen and smell the silence
I listen and embrace the silence.

◆ *From* **Summons to Life** by Martin Israel

The awareness of God is an awareness of warmth that permeates the very depth of our being. It speaks to us of power beyond thought that cares for us as we are, that loves us for what we are.

It is not that we feel greater love for others so much as that we are the receivers of ineffable love.

. . . The progressive revelation by the Holy Spirit, Who is deep within us in the spirit of the soul, leads us into an ever-deepening awareness of the divinity that lies at the heart of all creation and was supremely revealed in the juxtaposition of God and Man in the incarnational event. But if we are unwise enough to believe that we have the whole answer of God's being, we at once shut Him out of our lives, replacing Him with an idol, which may be theological, ritual, or intellectual, and which ultimately degenerates into a superstition.

On the other hand, the early revelations of God's love are as valid as the later ones. Nothing that is given at any time, that is truly God, can be anything but perfect. It is our own growth into awareness that enables God to come closer to us. The spiritual path becomes clear and defined when the personal God reveals Himself to us. This is our initiation into the life of the spirit.

◆ *From* **Collected Poems** by Rabindranath Tagore

Let thy love play upon my voice and rest on
my silence
Let it pass through my heart into all my movements.

Let thy love, like stars, shine in the darkness of
my sleep and dawn in my awakening.

Let it burn in the flame of my desires,
And flow in all currents of my own love.
Let me carry thy love in my life as a harp does its
music and give it back to thee at last with my life.

◆ *From* **Symbols and Dances** by Michael Stancliffe

Michael Stancliffe in a sermon with the text, 'A time to keep silence', said:

'We do not allow a place for silence, and we have no faith in the power of silence.' He goes on, 'Now I am not saying that we should not each of us speak to persuade others to accept what we honestly believe to be the truth. What I am saying is that before speaking there must be silence, and that what we say and how we say it, will come out of what we have learned in silence, about God, about ourselves and about those whom we are trying to help.

'It is in the silence that we shall be shown what we ought to say and how to say it.

'We cannot too often reflect upon the creative power of silence. We know that serious things have to be done in silence, because we do not have words to measure the immeasurable. In silence men pray, listen, compose, paint, write, think and suffer. These experiences are all occasions of giving and receiving, of some encounter with forces that are inexhaustible and independent of us.

'The invitation to discover our own meaning is extended to all. To each one of us He says:

I am the Way. Walk me.
I am the Truth. Sing me.
I am the Life. Live me.'

◆ *From* **With Pity Not With Blame** by Robert Llewelyn

Come
Holy Spirit. Spirit of Love, Spirit of Discipline.
In the silence.

COME to us and bring us Your Peace;
REST in us that we may be tranquil and still;
SPEAK to us as each heart needs to hear;
REVEAL to us things hidden and things longed for;
REJOICE in us that we may be at one with YOU and with each other;
REFRESH and RENEW us from your LIVING Spring of Water.

HOLY SPIRIT dwell in us that your LIGHT may shine through us, and that in our hearts you may find your homeliest home and endless dwelling.

◆ *From* **Christian Meditation** by John Main

God is our creator and our Father. Jesus is our Redeemer and our brother, and the Holy Spirit dwells within each one of us in such a way that we are, all of us, quite literally 'temples of holiness'.

Now meditation is simply the process whereby we come to terms with these truths, truths about God, truths about ourselves, truths about our neighbours. For in our own daily meditations we stand aside from all we can bring together under the term 'ephemeral immediacy' and open ourselves fully to the grandeur and the wonder of God – to the enduring present. And in this process we both discover our own grandeur and liberate our capacity for wonder. We might equally well say that in discovering our own value we discover God, the creator of all that is valuable. We discover with Gerard Manley Hopkins that 'the world is charged with the grandeur of God'.

In meditation we prepare for the full experience of the personal presence of Jesus within us, the personal presence of the Father, the Son and the Holy Spirit – the whole life of the most Holy Trinity lived out within us.

◆ ***Pope Paul VI*** during a visit to Poland

So let us leave aside words.
Let there remain just a great silence that turns into prayer.
I ask you to be with me on the White Mountain and in every other place.

There the communicated silence is a triangle formed of me, my friend and God.

◆ ***Dame Janet Baker*** *from* The Eric Symes Abbott Memorial Lecture, 1988

In music one of the most amazing influences on an audience is silence. The moment of complete silence in between two sounds can have an indescribable impact.

Most of us are talkers, we are eager to express our thoughts and opinions, the listener is in the minority.

The one able to offer silence is often the shy person, the one who thinks he has nothing to contribute to the conversation. Where would we talkers be without them I wonder.

The ability to listen, and listen non-judgementally, to someone who urgently needs a sympathetic ear is a vitally important aspect of ministry. Some of the most grievously sick people are people who, even in the midst of a loving family, are never properly heard, never listened to with compassion and understanding. So many of us are crying out for this kind of attention.

If you are the sort of person who can give it even though you may not feel able to advise, you have a talent and an avenue of personal ministry.

. . . We are light-bringers, pointing the way to hidden areas of the human spirit. Artists in their suffering, their vulnerability, their emotional commitment, express collectively the journey of the individual soul.

To deny the race the opportunity to witness the universal symbol is to deny the necessity of the individual expression of it: we are saying the individual does not need the idea of a soul.

◆ *From* **A Thousand Reasons for Living** by Dom Helder Camara

By the grace you grant me of silence without loneliness, give me the right to plead, to clamour for my brothers imprisoned in a loneliness without silence.

◆ *From* **With Open Hands** by Henri J.M. Nouwen

To pray means to open your hands before God. It means slowly relaxing the tension which squeezes your hands together and accepting your existence with an increasing readiness, not as a possession to defend but as a gift to receive.

Above all, therefore, prayer is a way of life which allows you to find stillness in the midst of the world. Where you open your hands to God's promises and find hope for yourself, your fellow men and the whole community in which you live. In prayer you encounter God in the soft breeze, in the distress of your neighbour and in the loneliness of your own heart.

◆ *From* **A Thousand Reasons for Living** by Dom Helder Camara

What will you say?
Look about you:
from the stars in their millions in the heights
to the stones, the water, to the animals, the plants,
you walk
among voiceless beings.
Look about you again
look
until you see the invisible
and you will tremble
at the silence of the angels
at the silence of God.

Speak then . . .

◆ *From* **Touch the Earth** by T.C. McLuhan

Ohiyesa, the Santec Dakote physician and author, speaks in 1911 about the manner in which his people worship.

'In the life of the Indian there was only one inevitable duty – the duty of prayer – the daily recognition of the Unseen and the Eternal. His daily devotions were more necessary to him than daily food. He wakes at daybreak, puts on his moccasins and steps down to the water's edge. Here he throws handfuls of clear cold water into his face, or plunges in bodily. After the bath he stands erect before the advancing dawn, facing the sun as it dances upon the horizon, and offers his unspoken orison. His mate may precede or follow him in his devotions, but never accompanies him. Each soul must meet the morning sun, the new sweet earth and the great silence alone.

'Whenever in the course of the daily hunt the red hunter comes upon a scene that is strikingly beautiful or sublime – a black thundercloud with the rainbow's glowing arch above a mountain, a white waterfall in the heart of a green gorge, a vast prairie tinged with the blood of sunset – he pauses for an instant in the attitude of worship. He sees no need for setting apart one day in seven as a holy day, since to him all days are God's.'

◆ ***Gestillte Sehnsucht***, Op.91, No. 1, by Ruckert (set to music by Brahms)

SILENT LONGING

Bathed in the golden glow of evening, how stately stand the woodlands. The soft blowing of the
evening breeze breathes in soft bird-voices. What are they whispering, the winds and the
birds? They are whispering the world to sleep.

Ye wishes, which always stir in my heart without
rest or peace. Thou longing which moves my soul
when wilt thou rest, when wilt thou slumber? Ye
yearning wishes, when will ye fall asleep to the
whispering of the winds and the birds?

When my spirit no longer hurries on the wings of
dreams into the golden distances: when my eyes
linger no more with longing glance at the eternal,
distant stars: then will the winds and the birds whisper
in harmony with my longing and my life.

◆ *From* **The Light Remains**, published by Glastonbury Abbey

JOHN KEATS

And then there crept
A little noiseless noise among the leaves,
Born of the very sigh that silence leaves.

◆ *From* **Light Within** by Laurence Freeman OSB

A sense of reverence is born in a gasp of wonder. Plato said that the love of wisdom begins with wonder. Wonder is also the condition of prayer which is a state of consciousness open to something greater than ourselves, not in fear, but in reverence and love. Wonder as the condition of prayer is not being baffled by not understanding; it is a state of certain knowledge and of clear vision. It is knowing by seeing intensely and wholly but it also involves knowing that what we see is part of the whole mystery.

The humility of the wonder of prayer is knowing that we have to open our consciousness further and that we can never know fully until we have transcended the last limits of our own consciousness to become one with the great consciousness that can be known only by its own self-knowledge.

Knowing what we see to be only a small part of the whole is still an exhilarating and enlivening experience. We know implicitly that we are expanding and that we will one day see the whole. We will know even as we are known. That is why, strange as it may sound, you can tell where there is real reverence by the presence of a spirit of joy. Reverence and wonder are expressed in the stillness and silence of meditation but from that stillness and silence comes the spirit of pure life, the bliss of God, the delight of spiritual knowledge. Liberty of spirit and a deeply rooted joy from the experience of wonder and our natural response of reverence fills us with a deep confidence.

◆ ***John Main*** OSB, *from* a tape recording

More and more thinking people in our society are coming to realise that the basic problems in our society are spiritual problems.

Not being content to live at one remove, not being content to read about it or to study it but to realise that the supreme reality is God, that God is love. To know this in your own heart.

All that is merely words unless we take practical steps to be open to the reality, that the spirit dwells in our hearts.

To allow God to unfold the mystery in your own heart, personally.

The purpose of saying the word *Ma-ra-na-tha* is to be free of all division, all disharmony. To be open to that supreme reality that God IS that God is LOVE.

◆ *From* **The Climate of Monastic Prayer** by Thomas Merton

This age which by its very nature is a time of crisis, of revolution and of struggle calls for the special searching and questioning which is the work of the Christian in silence, his meditation, his prayer; for he who prays searches not only his own heart but he plunges deep into the heart of the whole world in order to listen more intently to the deepest and most neglected voices that proceed from its inner depths.

◆ *From* **Touching Beauty's Hand** by Gwendy Caroe

When the wind sighs and urges
I must go,
Leave comfort, cups of tea, my care
And satisfaction, work or woe
And wander
Spirit-impelled or fairy led
Not asking where.

When earth's variety is held
In silver spell
I wait for airs that whispering come,
As message bringing; I cannot tell
The meaning –
Seeming from unknown land afar
Or spirit's home.

But when the world is hushed
And talking's ended,
With silence sinking layer on layer,
Quiet of earth and heaven blended,
Then must I pray
Seeking – not knowing how –
But needing prayer.

◆ *From* **Jean Vanier and l'Arche**, by Kathryn Spink

Sue Mosteller writes of her experiences at a Retreat taken by Jean Vanier:

'I was at a point in my religious life where I was searching because I was not finding. Jean called us to prayer. He called us to silence, and it was the first time in the whole of my religious life that I felt that silence was not empty, that it was full of the presence of God, that God was acting in my emptiness.

'There was a need in me, and that word came and filled the vacuum for me. I wanted to be more faithful, more radical.'

Three years later she would find herself at Daybreak, the first of the l'Arche communities in Canada.

◆ *From* **The Eye of the Eagle** by David Adam

What the desert Fathers and the Celtic saints showed was a richness of spirit amid their material poverty, a great sense of the eternal present in the passing of things transitory. They showed great poise at a time when many were falling apart. They carried within them a 'rest', an inner calm for which they became famous.

This inner calm *quies* is about the peace that passes all understanding, the peace which is a gift that comes with the Presence of God. They heeded and trusted the call. 'Come unto me and I will give you rest.' It was not an escape from the storms of life but a witness to the fact that we are not expected to face them alone. They sought to acknowledge that whatever the troubles which beset us, we are not left alone or forsaken. Far from being a place of impoverishment, the place of emptying can become the place where we are enriched. It is here that we can discover true and lasting values, and more important, here that we come to rely on our God. Instead of being the place of frantic searching it can be the place of rest and renewal.

We need to create the space that allows for the Divine, to make room in our lives, as the innkeeper made room in the stable – or He will be born elsewhere. It is only if we are willing to be alone with the Beloved that we can say we truly love Him. This will not decrease our love for the world for it is His creation, it will enhance it. It will not make us love our neighbours less, for we will see Him in them, and so respect them all the more. It will not diminish us as people but fulfil and enrich us. To leave behind all material things is to show that we want the heart-to-Heart encounter, and at the same time it shows that we know where our true riches lie.

. . . All your love, your stretching out, your hope, your thirst, God is creating in you so that He may fill you. It is not your desire that makes it happen, but His. He longs through your heart.

◆ ***George Appleton***

O Spirit of God, set at rest the crowded, hurrying, anxious thoughts within our minds and hearts.

Let the peace and quiet of Thy Presence take possession of us.

Help us to rest, to relax, to become open and receptive to Thee.

Thou dost know our inmost spirits, the hidden unconscious life within us, the forgotten memories of hurts and fears, the frustrated desires, the unresolved tensions and dilemmas.

Cleanse and sweeten the springs of our being that freedom, life and love may flow into both our conscious and hidden life.

Lord, we lie open before Thee, waiting for Thy peace, Thy healing and Thy word.

## SILENCE

◆ *From* **The Letters of Gertrude Bell, Volume I.**

THE SILENCE OF THE DESERT

My chief impression of the Desert. The Silence.

It is like the silence of the mountain tops, but more intense, for there you know the sound of the wind and far away water and falling ice and stones; there is a sort of echo of sound there, but here nothing.

◆ *From* **The Inner Christ** by John Main

There is no greater need in the Church and in the world today than for the renewed understanding that the call to prayer, to deep prayer is universal. Unity among Christians as well as in the long term, unity among different races and creeds rests upon our finding the inner principles of unity as a personal experience within our own hearts. If we are to realise that Christ is indeed the peace between us, we have to know that 'Christ is all and is in all'. And we in Him. The authority with which the Church communicates this experience will be the degree to which we, the Church and

Christ's Body, have realised it personally. Our authority has to be humble, that is it has to be rooted in an experience that takes us beyond ourselves into full personhood. Our authority as disciples is our closeness to the Author, far removed from authoritarianism or that complex of fear and guilt by which power is used by man against man. The Christian, in his prayer, renounces his own power. He leaves self behind. In so doing he places absolute faith in the power of Christ as the only power that increases the unity among men because it is the power of love, the power of union itself.

As Christian men or women of prayer open their hearts to this power they enlarge the capacity of all men to find the peace that lies beyond their ordinary understanding.

## ◆ *From* **Collected Papers of Evelyn Underhill**

### WHAT IS MYSTICISM?

The Christian mystic tries to continue in his own life Christ's balanced life of ceaseless communion with the Father and homely service to the crowd.

His love of God and thirst for God have been cleansed by long discipline from all self-interest; and the more profound his contemplation of God, the more he loves the world and tries to serve it as a tool of the divine creative love.

*I have included the following quotation as a tribute to Agatha Bathurst Norman.*

*Agatha was a disciple of Evelyn Underhill (herself a mystic), whom she knew well. After her death she carried on and expanded the way of led meditation she had learned from her teacher.*

*I know I can speak for all the members of the Fellowship of St Faith, started by Agatha, when I say how much we all owe to her for her leadership and guidance in this way of praying, the emphasis on silence and her introduction to the Prayer of Loving Attention. Aided and abetted by Dean Eric Abbott in his Westminster Abbey School of Prayer, together they introduced countless young people to the life of the spirit.*

*The quotation which follows Agatha wrote to her students on her retirement from King's College. E.B.*

◆ ***Agatha Bathurst Norman***, to her students on leaving King's College

This has been rather a strange session for me and I was thinking last night that I have felt rather like the Cheshire Cat in *Alice in Wonderland* for the circumstances have required a gradual fade out, and now we have got to the point where nothing is left but the grin.

But you remember perhaps if you are an Alice fan that Alice asked the Cheshire Cat before it faded out, 'Would you please tell me where I ought to go from here?' And the Cat replied, 'That depends a good deal on where you want to go to.' So before I fade out completely I want to say one last word about the importance of knowing where you want to get to.

It has been borne in on me, by my own experience and as the result of many conversations that I have had with Old Students, that however well-equipped one may be with academic degrees and qualifications, it is easy to lose one's sense of direction, to flounder about spiritually and be not only a burden to oneself but a stumbling block to other people. So I want my last word before I fade out to be this. Where do you want to get to? If you want to get to God, if you want to be used to get other people to God – and that is all that really matters – the way to go is the way of prayer. Don't neglect your prayers. There is nothing easier than to rationalise this neglect. School Assembly, preparing Scripture lessons (won't that do instead?) or we plead lack of time or spiritual loneliness. But when you start wandering off the track, come back, reset your compass, and God will help you. Whatever else you have not got time for, 'Stick to your prayers' and may God bless you all.

◆ ***Prayer of Dedication*** of the Christian Meditation Centre, 29 Campden Hill Road, London W8

May the Centre be a true spiritual home for the seeker, a friend for the lonely, a guide for the confused.

May those who teach here be strengthened by the Holy Spirit to serve all who come and to receive them as Christ Himself.

In the silence of this room may all the suffering, violence and confusion of the world encounter the power that will console, renew and uplift the human spirit.

May this silence be a power to open the hearts of men and women to the vision of God, and so to each other, in love and peace, justice and human dignity.

May the beauty of the Divine Life fill this house and the hearts of all who pray here, with joyful hope.

May all who come here, weighed down by the problems of humanity, leave, giving thanks for the wonder of human life.

We make this prayer through Christ our Lord.

◆ 6 ◆

# True Friendship

◆ ***George Eliot***

Oh the comfort, the inexpressible comfort of feeling safe with a person, having neither to weigh thoughts nor measure words, but pour them all out just as they are, chaff and grain together, knowing that a faithful hand will take and sift them, keep what is worth keeping and then with the breath of kindness, blow the rest away.

◆ *From* **The Best of Friends** by Hugh Whitemore

LETTER FROM DAME LAURENTIA MCLACHLAN TO SIR SYDNEY COCKERELL

What a mystery friendship is. And how strangely and delightfully different one's friends are one from the other – not only in themselves, but in the way one has to look at them. Some we have to carry, while others carry us. The perfect friend, to my mind, is one who believes in you once and for all and never requires explanations and assurances. True friendship is one of those subtle and beautiful forces that glorify life.

◆ *From* **The Best of Friends** by Hugh Whitemore

LETTER FROM DAME LAURENTIA MCLACHLAN TO SIR SYDNEY COCKERELL

Dear Sydney, What a gift and what a mystery our friendship is. It is one of those blessings that seem never to have had a beginning and which one feels are a part of one's very life. I suppose it was just waiting till we were ready for it. May it grow always into still deeper understanding until we are done with this earthly life, and may we come to perfect comprehension in eternal life, where I firmly believe all that is best in us will have fulfilment.

Do say Amen.

◆ *From* **The Review** by Brian Graham

TOUCH ME LORD

Touch me Lord, with Thy Comforting, Healing Presence, in those times when I feel lost and alone in the darkness of my night. Assure me in some small way that You are with me when the winds of adversity seek to extinguish the flame of my faith in You.

Touch me Lord, when I am down and sad, by the beauty of Your Presence in the flowers, trees and singing streams. In the rising and setting of the sun and in the brilliance of the stars, soft silver light of the moon. In the gentleness of animals and in the innocence of a child's heart.

Touch me Lord, through acts of human kindness and courage. In the positive aspect of right thinking and right speech. In the care and love that is given to those less fortunate than myself by many selfless souls the world over.

Touch me Lord, that I may truly value the gift You have given of my life and help me to give to others as I would like others to give to me. Help me to bring greater understanding and inspiration to those in need. Help me to dedicate my life in service to You, no matter how small my expression.

Touch me, Lord, with your Peace and Strength that I may not be afraid when facing the difficulties which life brings. Help me to see the blessings to be gained in overcoming my troubles and act on the greater wisdom and truth that is being revealed to me in such times.

Touch me Lord, through dance, movement, music and art which speaks of the noble nature of man and seeks to free my soul from my self-made prison. Help me walk forward into Your Light through the encircling gloom . . .

Eternal God, the power of Your Spirit pervades all creation. When we open our hearts to You, we are filled with Your strength to bear our afflictions, the strength to refuse them victory, the strength to overcome them.

◆ *From* **Meditations of the Heart** by H. Thurman

I share with you the agony of your grief
The anguish of your heart finds echo in

my own.
I know I cannot enter all you feel
Nor bear with you the burden of your pain,
I can but offer what my love does give
The strength of caring
The warmth of one who seeks to understand
The silent storm-swept barrenness of so great
a loss.
This I do in quiet ways
That on your lonely path
You may not walk alone.

*In our Journey, as we all know, we shall meet sorrow – our own deep sadness or that of someone we love or are concerned for. I am thinking now of spiritual healing, the healing of the bereaved, the healing quality in tears, in the shoulder to cry on, of what we can do to make ourselves channels for the healing grace which comes from God.*

*Peter Cornwell in* On the River's Edge *writes these helpful things to guide us. 'Although those in suffering and grief cry out "Why"? they are not in fact looking for a theoretical answer. No such answer, however neat and complete, would ease their pain. They look for healing, not knowledge. On the purely human level we see this happening not just in the obvious "happy ever after" way of health restored and success taking the place of failure, but also in those situations where there is no physical healing, no return of the child who has died. Even there, light comes and it comes from those who stand by and are willing to share something of the load. It is achieved by an act of human solidarity.*

*'. . . To move deliberately and with sensitivity into the orbit of suffering is costly, yet it is done daily by friends and good neighbours. Feeling tongue-tied and totally inadequate, they declare their solidarity with those in the darkness. The halting letter, the willingness to sit in silence – those are the gestures of readiness to touch the edges of suffering, just to be there. For all their apparent feebleness, the miracle is that those gestures bring light in a way which no neat answer to the question "Why?" could. Those who suffer know they are "as they say", upheld by such expression of solidarity.'*

◆ *From* **A Dusty Mirror: Thoughts and Poems** by Susan Wood

I would give you
The golden ball of the world
The glittering canopy of space,
If these would be your cure
And in my power to give.

But for your need
I offer all I have,
What have I for your comfort
But this poor human cloak,
Spread for you
Lovingly?

◆ *From* **The Vision of the Nazarene**, set down by the author of the Initiate

REAL CHARITY

Charitable are they who chancing on their wanderings to meet a sick or needy one, send out towards him a thought of health and love, for great is the power of love-charged thought; laudable is the secrecy of such an act.

O my Beloved, learn to feed other minds with the food of thy love-thoughts; for greatly canst thou benefit them, as also thyself.

◆ ***The White Eagle Lodge Prayer of Dedication***

May the light of Christ shining in my heart stand guard over my thought and guide my speech and actions into ways of service.

May the light of Christ shine from my heart
To heal the sick in mind and body;
To comfort the bereaved;
To sustain the weary.

May the light of Christ illume my understanding of all men, bringing true vision and awareness of the eternal life, and of the Christ within all mankind.

◆ ***The Power of the Powerless*** by Jürgen Moltmann

It is only the person who knows loneliness and doesn't flee from it who can hold community with the lonely.

It is only the person who knows the frontier where all human help fails, who can stand by the helpless.

It is only the person who knows the guilt that no one can make good, who can remain beside the guilty.

It is only the person who has made dying as part of his life and no longer repressed it, who can accompany the dying.

O Lord who knowest the needs of every heart, look in mercy on those who are beyond human help, all whose hope is gone and all whose sickness finds no cure, all who feel beaten by the storms of life.

Grant them Thy strength and uphold them with Thy love.

And now all through the days may we touch as many lives as Thou wouldst have us touch for Thee; and those we touch do Thou with Thy Holy Spirit quicken, whether by the word we speak, the letter we write, or the prayer we breathe, or the life we live.

The Grace of our Lord Jesus Christ and the love of God and the fellowship of the Holy Ghost be with us all evermore.

◆ ***The Beatitudes for Friends of the Handicapped*** by Bob Lindsay

Blessed are you who take time to listen to difficult speech, for you help us to know that if we persevere we can be understood.

Blessed are you who walk with us in public places and ignore the stares of strangers for in your companionship we find havens of relaxation.

Blessed are you who never bid us to 'hurry up' and more blessed you who do not snatch our tasks from us, for often we need time rather than help.

Blessed are you who stand beside us when we enter new and untried ventures for our failures will be outweighed by the times we surprise ourselves and you.

Blessed are you who ask for our help, for our greatest need is to be needed.

Blessed are you who helped us with the graciousness of Christ, for often we need the help we cannot ask for.

Blessed are you when by all these things you assure us that the thing that makes us individuals is not in our peculiar muscles, nor in our wounded nervous systems, but in the God-given self that no infirmity can confine.

Rejoice and be exceedingly glad and know that you give us reassurance that could never be spoken in words, for you deal with us as God has dealt with all his children.

◆ ***Lord When I am Hungry***, translated from the French *Prières pour une Foi*

Lord when I am hungry
Give me someone to feed,
When I am thirsty
Give water for their thirst.

When I am sad
Someone to lift from sorrow,
When burden weighs upon me
Lay upon my shoulders
The burden of my fellows.

Lord when I stand
Greatly in need of tenderness,
Give me someone who yearns for love.
May your will
Be my bread; your grace
My strength; your love
My resting place.

◆ ***The Reverend Samuel Longfellow*** (1819–1892)

Into all our lives, in many simple, familiar, homely ways, God infuses this element of joy from the surprises of life, which unexpectedly brighten our days and fill our lives with light.

He drops this added sweetness into our cup and makes it to run over. The success we were not counting on, the blessing we were not trying after, the strains of music in the midst of drudgery, the beautiful morning picture or sunset glory thrown in as we pass to or from our daily business, the unsought word of encouragement or expression of sympathy, the sentence that meant for us more than the writer or speaker thought. These and one hundred others that everyone's experience can supply are instances of what I mean.

You may call it accident or chance – it often is; you may call it human goodness – it often is.

But always, always call it God's love, for that is always in it. These are the overflowing riches of His grace, these are His free gifts.

◆ ***Wedding Prayer***

Heavenly Father, we offer you our souls and bodies, our thoughts and words and deeds, our love for one another.

Unite our wills in your will, that we may grow together in love and peace all the days of our life;

Through Jesus Christ our Lord. Amen.

◆ *From* **A Thousand Reasons for Living** by Dom Helder Camara

It is worth any sacrifice, however great or costly, to see eyes that were listless light up again; to see someone smile who seemed to have forgotten how to smile, to see trust reborn in someone who no longer believed in anything or anyone.

◆ ***Hosea 2:3–4***

Yet it was I who taught Ephraim to walk.
  I took them up in my arms;
  but they did not know that I healed them.
I led them with the cords of compassion,
  with the bonds of love,
and I became to them as one
  who eases the yoke on their jaws
and I bent down to them and fed them.

◆ ***Footprints***, author unknown

One night a man had a dream. He dreamed that he was walking along the beach with the Lord.

Across the sky flashed scenes from his life. For each scene, he noticed two sets of footprints in the sand: one belonging to him and the other to the Lord.

When the last scene of his life flashed before him, he looked back at the footprints in the sand. He noticed that many times along the path of his life there was only one set of footprints. He also noticed that it happened at the very lowest and saddest times of his life.

This really bothered him and he questioned the Lord about it. 'Lord, you said that once I decided to follow you, you'd walk with me all the way. But I have noticed that during the most troublesome times in my life, there is only one set of footprints. I don't understand why, when I needed you most, you would leave me.'

The Lord replied, 'My son. My precious child, I love you and would never leave you. During your times of trial and suffering, when you saw only one set of footprints, it was then that I carried you.'

◆ ***Four-Feet*** by Rudyard Kipling

I have done mostly what most men do
And pushed it out of my mind;
But I can't forget if I wanted to,
Four-Feet running behind.

Day after day, the whole day through –
Wherever my road inclined –
Four-Feet said 'I am coming with you'
And trotted along behind.

Now I must go by some other round –
Which I shall never find –
Somewhere that does not carry the sound
Of Four-Feet trotting behind.

◆ 7 ◆

# The Journey's End

Sunset and evening star

*Lord Tennyson*

◆ *From* **More Latin Lyrics** translated by Helen Waddell

THOMAS AQUINAS

The Word went forth
    Yet from his Father never went away,
Came to his work on earth,
    And laboured till the twilight of his day.

Men envied him: He went to death
    By his own men betrayed
But first to his own men himself had given
    In wine and broken bread.

In birth he gave himself to men,
    At meat their holy bread
Dying he gave himself their ransoming:
    Reigning their high reward.

O Victim slain for us and our salvation
    Opening the doors of light
The warring hosts are set on our damnation
    Give us the strength to fight.

◆ *From* **More Latin Lyrics** translated by Helen Waddell

ALCUIN
ON THE CROSS

Here dying for the world, the world's life hung.
    Laving a world's sin in that deathly tide:

That downbent head raised earth above the skies
    O timeless wonder! Life because one died.

◆ *Dietrich Bonhoeffer from* **Letters and Papers from Prison**

CHRISTIANS AND PAGANS

Men go to God when they are sore bestead,
Pray to him for succour, for his peace, for bread,
For mercy for them sick, sinning, or dead,
All men do so, Christian and unbelieving.

Men go to God when he is sore bestead,
Find him poor and scorned, without shelter or bread,
Whelmed under weight of the wicked, the weak, the dead;
Christians stand by God in his hour of grieving.

God goes to every man when sore bestead,
Feeds body and spirit with his bread,
For Christians, pagans alike he hangs dead,
And both alike forgiving.

◆ *From* **The Songs of the Lover and the Beloved**, translated from the Spanish and Catalan by E. Allison Peers

TO CHRIST CRUCIFIED

I am not moved, my God to love of Thee
By Heaven which Thou dost pledge me as reward.
I am not moved to cease to grieve Thee, Lord
By thoughts and fears of Hell which threaten me.
Thou mov'st me, O my God mov'd sore am I,
To see Thee nailed upon that cruel Tree,
The scorn of men, wounded despitefully
Mov'd am I: Thou dost suffer and dost die
Mov'd am I thus, my Lord to love Thee yea
Were there no Heaven at all I'd love Thee still,
Were there no Hell, my due of fear I'd pay,
Thou need'st not make me gifts to move my will
For were my hopes of Heaven quite fled away,
Yet this same love my heart would ever fill.

◆ *Charles Wesley from* **Uncommon Prayers**, collected by Cecil Hunt

Love Divine, all loves excelling.

◆ *An Ancient Moslem Prayer*

O my Lord. If I worship Thee from fear of hell, burn me in hell; and if I worship Thee from hope of Paradise, exclude me thence; but if I worship Thee for Thine own sake, then withhold not from me Thine Eternal Beauty.

## THE RESURRECTION

◆ *From* **French manuscript**, Oxford Carols, no. 119

Now the green blade riseth from the buried grain,
Wheat that in dark earth many days had lain.
Love lives again, that with the dead has been:
Love is come again, like wheat that springeth green.

In the grave they laid Him, love whom men had slain,
Thinking that never He would wake again.
Lain on the earth like grain that slept unseen
Love is come again, like wheat that springeth green.

Forth He came at Easter, like the risen grain.
He that for three days in the grave had lain,
Quick from the dead my risen Lord is seen
Love is come again, like wheat that springeth green.

When our hearts are wintry, grieving or in pain,
Thy touch can call us back to life again,
Fields of our hearts that dead and bare have been:
Love is come again, like wheat that springeth green.

◆ *From* **More Latin Lyrics** translated by Helen Waddell

I shall not go to heaven when I die.
    But if they let me be,
I think I'll take a road I used to know
    That goes by Shere-na-garagh and the sea.
And all day breasting me the winds will blow,

And I'll hear nothing but the peewit's cry
And the waves talking in the sea below.

I think it will be winter when I die
For no one from the north could die in spring –
And so the heather will be green and grey:
And the bog-cotton will have blown away
And there will be no yellow on the whin.

And I shall smell the peat,
And when it's almost dark I'll set my feet
Where a white track goes glimmering to the hills,
And I see far up a light –
Do you think heaven could be so small a thing
As a lit window on the hill at night?

And come in stumbling from the gloom
Half blind, into a firelit room
Turn and see you
And there abide.
If it were true
And I thought that they would let me be,
I almost wish it were tonight I died.

◆ *From* **A Dusty Mirror: Thoughts and Poems** by Susan Wood

POLITICAL PRISONER

Here is the leaping light
The great spaces of the sea,
And air blown down
The long corridors of the earth.

There is no space
But one encirclement
Of stone on stone
And the dull ooze of damp in grey seams.

Here, is light breaking with each wave
Light flowing from the sky

Free limbs air-wrapped
Sun embalmed.

There, is darkness
An absence of light,
So permanent, no night nor day
Exist, but one long dark.

Here is the winged silence of the air
The silence of deep water
Silence full of the sounds of living
The sound of the stars passing.

There is a silence so dead as to make
A voice sound cracked and crazy
Listening to itself,
The silence of being buried alive.

I full of riches
In the midst of life
Know the extreme comfort
Of the touch and feel and sound
Of those I love.

While he, grave, emaciated
Cut off from all things living
Deprived of all but life
Communes with insects
Giving his life blood
To a mosquito

As to a friend.

Can it be the same life,
Can we be living in the same world?
Or is there a greater distance
Between life and life,
Than between the living and the dead?

◆ *From* **A Fragment of a Sermon** by Lidden of St Paul's, speaking on the first five minutes after death.

At our entrance in another world we shall know our old selves as never before. The past will be spread out before us, we shall take a comprehensive survey of it. Each man's life will be displayed to him as a river, which he traces from its source till it mingles with the distant ocean. The course of that river lies sometimes through dark forests which hide it from view, sometimes through sands or marshes in which it seems to lose itself. Here it forces its passage angrily between rocks, then it glides gently through meadows.

At one time it might seem to be turning backward out of caprice, at another to be parting with half its volume of water like a spendthrift, while later it receives new streams that restore its strength. And so it passes on till the ebb and flow of the tides on its bank tells that the end is near.

What will not the retrospect be when after death we survey for the first time the whole scene – the strange vicissitudes, the loss and gain, the failures and the triumphs of our earthly existence? Those first five minutes, that first awakening to a new existence, will only be tolerable if we have indeed with the hands of faith and love, laid hold of the faith hope set before us, in the person of Jesus Christ our Lord and Saviour. We may then think calmly even of that tremendous experience if the eternal God is our refuge – and underneath are the everlasting arms.

◆ ***We Can No Longer See You*** by Virginia Thesiger

We can no longer see you
You make no sound.
The world believes you have 'gone on'
somewhere.
Theories abound.

Where could you go?
Our lively, lovely friend?
For God is the life of man
Without start or end.

God holds His world complete,
in its life we share,
there is nowhere out of this world to go:
no here or there.

Ours, only ours the blindness,
ours is the road to take
(through the mists and the myths and the
laws that part
and the hearts that break).

Into that still, small place
where illusion's done
and we find that you, us, and all
with God are one.

◆ *From* **Bartlett's Familiar Quotations**, compiled by John Bartlett, written by William Ewart Gladstone (Little Brown & Co, 1882)

Tell him, oh gracious Lord if it may be how much I love him and miss him and long to see him again, and if there be ways in which he may come, vouchsafe him to me as a guard and guide and grant me a sense of his nearness in such degree as thy love permits.

◆ ***To My Son*** by Dorothea Eastwood

Son, I am powerless to protect you: though
My heart for yours beats ever anxiously,
Blind through piteous darkness you must go,
And find with new vision sights I see.
If it might ease you I would bear again
All the old suffering that I too have known.
All sickness, terror, and the spirit's pain,
But you, alas, must make these three your own.

Yes, though I bear away a thousand fears
And forge your armour without flaw or chink,
And though I batter heaven with my prayers,
Yet from a self-filled cup of grief you drink,

Oh, son of woman, since I gave you breath
You walk alone to face your death.

◆ *From* **The Dream of Gerontius** by Cardinal Newman (set to music by Edward Elgar)

I went to sleep; and now I am refreshed
A strange refreshment: for I feel in me
An inexpressive lightness, and a sense
Of freedom as I were at length myself,
and ne'er had been before. How still it is!
I hear no more the busy beat of time.
No, nor my fluttering breath, nor struggling pulse;
Nor does one moment differ from the rest.

The silence pours a solitariness
Into the very essence of my soul;
And the deep rest, so soothing and so sweet,
Hath something too of sternness and of pain.
Another marvel: someone has me fast
Within his ample palm. A uniform
And gentle pressure tells me I am not
Self-moving, but borne forward on my way
And hark! I hear a singing: yet in sooth
I cannot of that music rightly say
Whether I hear or touch or taste the tones.
Oh, what a heart-subduing melody.

◆ Rabbi Hugo Gryn *from* **The Daily Telegraph**, Thursday 22nd October 1987

THE FUNERAL SERVICE FOR
JACQUELINE DU PRÉ

When we are dead and people weep for us and grieve, let it be because we touched their lives with beauty and simplicity.

Let it not be said that life was good to us but rather we were good to life.

◆ *From* **The Undiscovered Country** by Robert Morgan

SENECA TO MARCIA: ON CONSOLATION

Throughout the free and boundless spaces of eternity they wander, no intervening seas block their course: no lofty mountains or pathless valleys or shallows of the shifting Syrtes: their every way is level and being swift and unencumbered, they easily are pervious to the matter of the stars and in turn are mingled with it.

◆ *From* **Touch the Earth: A Self-Portrait of Indian Existence**, compiled by T.C. McLuhan

Dying words of Crowfoot, a great hunter, brave warrior and eloquent spokesman, in what is now Alberta province.

His last words were of life.

> 'What is life? It is the flash of a firefly in the Night. It is the breath of a buffalo in the winter time. It is the little shadow which runs across the grass and loses itself in the Sunset.'

◆ ***The Death of the Bird*** by A.D. Hope

For every bird there is this last migration:
Once more the cooling year kindles her heart;
With a warm passage to the summer station
Love pricks the course in lights across the chart.

Year after year a speck on the map, divided
By a whole hemisphere, summons her to come;
Season after season, sure and safely guided,
Going away she is also coming home.

And being home, memory becomes a passion
With which she feeds her brood and straws her nest,
Aware of ghosts that haunt the heart's possession
And exiled love mourning within her breast.

The sands are green with a mirage of valleys;
The palm tree casts a shadow not its own;

Down the long architrave of temple or palace
Blows a cool air from moorland scarps of stone.

And day by day the whisper of love grows stronger;
That delicate voice, more urgent with despair
Custom and fear consuming her no longer
Drives her at last on the waste leagues of air.

A vanishing speck on those inane dominions
Single and frail, uncertain of her place
Alone in the bright host of her companions
Lost in the blue unfriendliness of space.

She feels it close now the appointed season
The invisible thread is broken as she flies
Suddenly without warning, without reason
The guiding spark of instinct winks and dies.

Try as she will, the trackless world delivers
No way, the wilderness of light no sign
The immense and complex map of hills and rivers
Mocks her small wisdom with its vast design.

And darkness rises from the eastern valleys,
And the winds buffet her with their hungry breath
And the great earth, with neither grief nor malice
Receives the tiny burden of her death.

◆ *From* **Letters of Gertrude Bell, Volume I.**

DIVAN OF HAFIZ XIV: FROM POEM ON THE DEATH OF HIS SON

The nightingale with drops of his heart's blood
Had nourished the red rose, then came a wind,
And catching at the boughs in envious mood,
A hundred thorns about his heart entwined,
Like to the parrot crunching sugar, good
Seemed the world to me who could not stay
The wind of Death that swept my hopes away.

Light of mine eyes, and harvest of my heart,
And mine at least in changeless memory!
Ah! when he found it easy to depart,
He left the harder pilgrimage to me!
Oh Camel-driver, though the cordage start,
For God's sake help me lift my fallen load
And Pity be my comrade on the road.

. . . He sought a lodging in the grave too soon!
I had not castled, and the time is gone,
What shall I play? Upon the chequered floor
Of Night and Day, Death won the game – forlorn
And careless now, Hafiz can lose no more.

◆ ***A Prayer for one who took his own life***

O God righteous and compassionate
Forgive the despair of . . . for whom we pray.
Heal in him that which is broken,
And in your great love stand with those
Hurt by the violence of his end.
Lord be to him not a judge but a Saviour
Receive him into that Kingdom wherein by your mercy
We sinners also would have place
Through the merits of our wounded Redeemer
Who lives and reigns with you in the Holy Spirit
Power now and unto the Ages of Ages.

◆ *From* **Letters of Gertrude Bell, Volume I** selected by Lady Bell

Gertrude was an ardent lover of poetry all her life long. She seemed, after the book of Hafiz whose poems she translated had appeared, to consider her own gift of verse as a secondary approach and to our surprise abandoned it altogether. But that gift has always seemed to me to underlie all she has written. The spirit of poetry coloured all her prose descriptions, all the pictures that she herself saw and succeeded in making others see.

She published a translation of the Divan of Hafiz in 1897. The book included a life of Hafiz which is practically a history of his time as well as a critical study of his work . . . She draws a parallel between Hafiz and his contemporary Dante: she notes the similarity of a passage with Goethe, she compares Hafiz with Villon, on every side gathering fructifying examples which link together the inspiration of the West and the East.

TO HAFIZ OF SHIRAZ

Thus said the Poet: 'When death comes to you
All ye whose life-sand through the hour glass slips
He lays two fingers on your ears and two
Upon your eyes, he lays one on your lips,
Whispering: "Silence". Although deaf thine ears
Thine eyes, my Hafiz Time's eclipse.
The songs thou sangest still all men may hear.

'Songs of dead laughter songs of love once hot,
Songs of a cup once flushed rose-red with wine,
Songs of a rose whose beauty is forgot
A nightingale that piped hushed lays divine
And still a graver music runs beneath
The tender love notes of those songs of thine
Oh Seeker of the keys of Life and Death.'

◆ *From* **Cymbeline** by William Shakespeare

SONG

Fear no more the heat o' the sun,
    Nor the furious winter's rages;
Thou thy worldly task hast done,
    Home art gone and ta'en thy wages:
Golden lads and girls all must,
    As chimney-sweepers, come to dust.

Fear no more the frown o' the great;
    Thou art past the tyrant's stroke:
Care no more to clothe and eat;
    To thee the reed is as the oak:
The sceptre, learning, physic, must
    All follow this, and come to dust.

Fear no more the lightning-flash,
    Nor the all-dreaded thunder-stone;
Fear not slander, censure rash;
    Thou hast finish'd joy and moan:
All lovers young, all lovers must
    Consign to thee, and come to dust.

No exorciser harm thee!
    Nor no witchcraft charm thee!
Ghost unlaid forbear thee!
    Nothing ill come near thee!
Quiet consummation have;
    And renowned be thy grave!

◆ ***From Jeremiah 31:12***

And their soul shall be as a watered garden and they shall not sorrow any more.

◆ ***For Dr Patricia Graeme***

Written for her by the grateful relative of a patient for whom she had cared.

She writes with the hand of life
To the land of the living.
She writes with gentleness of death's strife
To the land of the loving.
She writes of death with the hand of life
To those who are grieving.
She writes of the spirit alive and unending
She brings sweetness to the living.

◆ *From* **Poems** by John Donne 1633

A HYMN TO GOD THE FATHER, 1633

Wilt thou forgive that sin where I begun,
    Which was my sin, though it were done before?
Wilt thou forgive that sin through which I run,
    And do run still, though still I do deplore?

When thou hast done, thou hast not done,
For I have more.

Wilt thou forgive that sin which I have won
Others to sin and made my sin their door?
Wilt thou forgive that sin which I did shun
A year or two, but wallowed in a score?
When thou hast done, thou hast not done,
For I have more.

I have a sin of fear, that when I have spun
My last thread, I shall perish on the shore;
But swear by thyself that at my death thy Son
Shall shine as he shines now and heretofore;
And having done that, Thou hast done,
I have no more.

*Bishop John Taylor writes in the 'Primal Vision' of the importance of keeping in touch with those we love in that other world through prayer, remembering them and asking them to remember us.*

*'Surely the "tender bridge" that joins the living with the dead in Christ is prayer. Mutual intercession is the life-blood of this fellowship, and what is there in Christian death that can possibly check its flow? To ask for the prayers of others in this life and to know that they rely on mine does not show any lack of faith in the all-sufficiency of God. Then in the same faith let me ask for their prayers still, and offer mine for them, even when death has divided us. They pray for me, may I believe, with clearer understanding but I for them in ignorance though still with love, and love not knowledge is the substance of prayer. It is not right that this natural expression of Christian love be confined to members of the Church. One of the commonest questions asked of ministers in times of bereavement is how the widow or widower is to think of husband or wife who was not a member of the Church or even an attender at its worship. The answer is simply that death does not kill love, in some ways it deepens it. Love wants to express itself without inhibition, in prayer and faith.*

*The words "in Adam all . . ." includes the whole family of Man, in death, the promise "in Christ all" cannot include less than that in life.'*

*From 2nd Maccabees, 1:3–5.*

*'God give us all a heart to serve him and do his will with a good courage and a willing mind and send us peace and hear our prayers, and be at one with us and never forsake us in time of trouble.'*

◆ *From* **More Latin Lyrics** translated by Helen Waddell

Boethius' definition of eternity: 'The possession of all time past, present, and to come, in full plenitude, in one single moment, here and now.'

◆ ***J. Ellerton*** *from* **The English Hymnal**, no. 277

The day thou gavest, Lord, is ended,
    The darkness falls at thy behest;
To thee our morning hymns ascended,
    Thy praise shall sanctify our rest.

We thank thee that thy Church unsleeping,
    While earth rolls onward into light,
Through all the world her watch is keeping,
    And rests not now by day or night.

As o'er each continent and island
    The dawn leads on another day,
The voice of prayer is never silent,
    Nor dies the strain of praise away.

The sun that bids us rest is waking
    Our brethren 'neath the western sky,
And hour by hour fresh lips are making
    Thy wondrous doings heard on high.

So be it, Lord; thy throne shall never,
    Like earth's proud empires, pass away;
Thy kingdom stands, and grows for ever,
    Till all thy creatures own thy sway.

◆ ***Rabindranath Tagore***

Death is putting out the Lamp because the Dawn has come.

# ACKNOWLEDGEMENTS

The compiler acknowledges with gratitude the courtesy of those publishers, other organisations and individuals who have given special permission for us to use extracts from their copyright material, and our thanks are also due to others whose copyright material has been included in this book.

All Hallows by the Tower for 'A Life in Your Hands' by Dorothy Law Holte; Amber Lane Press for *The Best of Friends* by Hugh Whitemore © 1988 Stanbrook Abbey; l'Arche for 'A Wound Deep in the Heart' by Jean Vanier; Arthur James for *Creative Silence* by Denis Duncan and *God Calling: A Devotional Diary by Two Listeners* edited by A. J. Russell; Ave Maria Press, Indiana, USA, for *With Open Hands* by Henri J. M. Nouwen. Copyright 1972 by Ave Maria Press Inc., Notre Dame, IN 46556. All rights reserved; Cassell PLC for *Anglican Spirituality* by Canon William Purcell; Christian Meditation Centre for 'Disclosure' by Ann Lewin; for their Prayer of Dedication and for *Christian Meditation* by John Main; Constable and Co Ltd for *More Latin Lyrics* by Helen Waddell; Darton, Longman and Todd for 'Light as the Glory of God', *A Glimpse of Glory* by Gonville ffrench-Beytagh; *Bread of the World* by John Hadley; *In Search of a Way* and *Walk to Jerusalem* by Gerard Hughes; *The Inner Christ* and *Moment of Christ* by John Main; *With Pity Not with Blame* by Robert Llewelyn; *Jean Vanier and l'Arche* by Kathryn Spink; *The Universal Christ: Daily Readings with Bede Griffiths* edited by Peter Spink; *On the River's Edge* by Peter Cornwell; The C. W. Daniel Co Ltd for *The Gate of Healing* by Dr Pearce; The Dovecote Press for *David Cecil: A Portrait by His Friends* by Hannah Cranbourne; David Higham Associates for 'Morning has Broken', from *The Children's Bells* by Eleanor Farjeon; Faber and Faber Ltd for extracts from *Season*

*Songs*, *Hawk in the Rain*, *Wodwo* and *Poetry in the Making*, all by Ted Hughes and *Collected Poems* by Edwin Muir; Hamish Hamilton Ltd for *The Land Unknown* by Kathleen Raine; HarperCollins Publishers for George MacDonald Autobiography by C. S. Lewis; *Morning has Broken* by Richard Harries; *Being in Love* by William Johnston; *Journey to Ladakh* (paperback) by Andrew Harvey. (Thanks are due also to Jonathan Cape for *Journey to Ladakh*.); Hodder & Stoughton Ltd for *Summons to Life* by Martin Israel; *The Undiscovered Country* by Robert Morgan and several prayers from *Uncommon Prayers*, collected by Cecil Hunt; The Literary Trustees of Walter De La Mare and the Society of Authors as their representative for 'The Scribe' by Walter De La Mare; Loretta Barrett Books Inc. and the author for *Touch the Earth* by T. C. McLuhan; Julia MacRae Books and Dame Janet Baker for *Full Circle* by Janet Baker; Methuen Children's Books for *The Tao of Pooh* by Benjamin Hoff; John Murray for *Moments of Vision* by Kenneth Clark; Priscilla Napier for 'The Kingdom of Edmund'; The Office of H.R.H. The Prince of Wales for *The Earth in Balance* (BBC Television); Oxford University Press for The *Oxford Book of Carols*; *God as Spirit* by G. W. H. Lampe and *The Spiritual Nature of Man* by Alistair Hardy; Penguin Books for *Weavers of Wisdom: Women Mystics of the Twentieth Century* by Anne Bancroft; Laurence Pollinger and the Estate of Frieda Lawrence Ravagli for 'Bare Almond Trees' by D. H. Lawrence; The Quaker Press, Religious Society of Friends, for 'Lord When I Am Hungry'; *The Review* (formerly *The Science of Thought Review*), The Science of Thought Press Ltd, for 'Touch Me, Lord' and A Song, My Lord' by Brian Graham; SCM Press Ltd for the poem 'Christians and Pagans' from Dietrich Bonhoeffer, *Letters and Papers from Prison*, The Enlarged Edition (1971), and for *Christianity Rediscovered* by Vincent J. Donovan; Scottish Academic Press for 'Rest Benediction' (a Celtic Prayer) from *Carmina Gadelica Vol. 3* (Quoted in *The Eye of the Eagle* by David Adam (SPCK); Search Press/Burns and Oates Ltd for *The Cosmic Christ* by Ladislaus Boros; Sheed & Ward for *The Complete Works of St Teresa*, translated by E. Allison Peers; Sheldon Press for *The Garden of the Beloved* by Robert Way; S. J. Publishers, Ananda, India, for *The Song of the Bird* by Anthony de Mello; SLG Press for an extract from *The Simplicity of Prayer: Extracts from the Teaching of Mother Mary Clare SLG*; Mary Spain for 'A Quickening Joy'; SPCK for extracts from *The Eye of the Eagle* (1990) by David Adam; *Symbols and Dances* (1986) and *Jacob's Ladder* by Michael Stancliffe; St Mary's Abbey, West Malling for 'Hymn for Terce', 'Prayer', and *Exploration into Love*, and for the prayer for one who took his own life; Virginia Thesiger for 'To a Villain'; 'A Call to Birds of a Feather' and 'We Can No Longer See You'; The White Eagle Publishing Trust for the White Eagle Lodge Prayer of Dedication; Susan Wood for *From a Dusty Mirror Thoughts and Poems*; World Congress of Faiths for the Sir Francis Younghusband Memorial Lecture, 28th May 1986, by Robert Runcie.

Most of the hymns in this volume appear in the *English Hymnal*; many are also to be found in a variety of other hymnbooks, including *Hymns Ancient and Modern*. The version of the Bible most commonly quoted is the Revised Standard Version, copyrighted 1971 and 1952 by the Division of Christian Education of the National Council of Churches of Christ in the USA.

The compiler and publishers of this book have made every endeavour to trace the copyright owners of each extract. There do, however, remain a small number of short extracts for which the source is unknown to the compiler and publishers. The publishers would be glad to hear from the copyright owners of these extracts and due acknowledgement will be made in all future editions of the book.

# INDEX OF AUTHORS

Adam, David 51, 86, 118, 141
Appleton, George 10, 74, 142
Arab Chieftan, A 31
Augustine, St 3, 129

Baker, Janet 114, 116, 135
Bancroft, Anne 131, 132
Behr, Aby 82
Bell, Gertrude 142, 168, 169
Berlin, Isaiah 115
Black Elk 58
Bonhoeffer, Dietrich 160
Boros, Ladislaus 97
Braybrook, Marcus 74
Browne, Sir Thomas 6
Browning, Elizabeth Barrett 94

Camara, Dom Helder 7, 58, 136, 137, 155
Caroe, Gwendy 29, 140
Clark, Kenneth 105

de Mello, Anthony 13, 15
De Tourville, The Abbé 68, 76
De La Mare, Walter 30, 47
Dhu'l-Nun 16
Donne, John 171
Donovan, Vincent J. 9
Duncan, Denis 128

Eastwood, Dorothea 5, 35, 40, 46, 114, 119, 165
Eliot, George 149
Ellerton, J. 173
Emerson, Ralph Waldo 34

Faber, F. W. 98
Farjeon, Eleanor 31
ffrench-Beytagh, Gonville 16
Foster, Richard J. 108
Freeman, Laurence 138

Garvin, Viola 6
General Conference of American Rabbis 88
Gilmore, Mary 21, 32
Gladstone, William Ewart 165
Goethe 67
Graham, Brian 80, 150
Griffiths, Bede 73

Hadley, John 17, 18, 23, 76, 77, 86
Hardy, Alistair 93
Harries, Richard 3
Harvey, Andrew 78, 79
Hoff, Benjamin 112
Holte, Dorothy Law 101
Hope, A. D. 167
Hopkins, Gerard Manley 52
Hughes, Gerard 17, 27, 42, 65, 66
Hughes, Ted 36, 39, 49, 54, 109, 117
Hunt, Cecil 82

Irvine, Gerald 113
Israel, Martin 133

John XXIII, Pope 80
Johnston, William 24

Keats, John 138
Kipling, Rudyard 156
Knatchbull-Hugesen, Edward 44

Lampe, G. W. H. 9, 14
Law, William 94
Law-Smith, Joan 22
Lawrence, D. H. 85, 87
Lewin, Ann 59
Lidden of St Paul's 164
Lindsay, Bob 153
Llewelyn, Robert 134
Longfellow, Henry 82, 92
Longfellow, Samuel 154

MacArthur, General Douglas 113
MacDonald, George 43, 80
MacQuarrie, John 22
Main, John 73, 125, 130, 135, 139, 142
Mary Clare, Mother 66
Masefield, John 28
McLuhan, T. C. 56, 57, 130, 137, 167
Menuhin, Yehudi 116
Merton, Thomas 132, 139
Mitchell, Anna Margaret 40
Moltmann, Jürgen 153
Morgan, Robert 167
Muir, Edwin 89, 110

Napier, Priscilla 99
Newbolt, Sir Henry 106
Newman, John Henry 50, 166
Norman, Agatha Bathurst 144
Nouwen, Henri J. M. 136

Olrik, Axel 100

Paul VI, Pope 135
Pearce, Ian 70
Peers, E. Allison 160
Prince of Wales, H.R.H. The 25
Pritchard, Rowland Hugh 14
Purcell, William 64

Quoist, Michel 127

Raine, Kathleen 10
Rees, Timothy 14
Riches, John 7
Ridding, Bishop 71
Robinson, J. Armitage 43
Roose-Evans, James 69, 129
Ruckert 138
Runcie, Robert 71, 93
Russell, A. J. 12
Russell, George 107
Ruysbroek, Johannes 53

Sassoon, Siegfried 3
Sears, E. H. 38
Seneca Indian Historical Society 25
Shakespeare, William 37, 170
Shelley, Percy Bysshe 30
Smith, Julia 110
Spain, Mary 26
Spink, Kathryn 140
Stancliffe, Michael 89, 134

Tagore, Rabindranath 45, 65, 131, 133, 175
Temple, Archbishop William 4
Tennyson, Lord 46, 157
Thesiger, Virginia 83, 164
Thomas, R. S. 28
Thurman, H. 150
Traherne, Thomas 90
Trine, Ralph Waldo 96, 117

Underhill, Evelyn 56, 143
Union of Progressive Synagogues 11

Vanier, Jean 84, 106
Verdon, Bryony 53

Waddell, Helen 8, 32, 159, 161, 173
Ward, Keith 119
Waugh, Evelyn 67
Way, Robert 29
Wesley, Charles 160
Whitemore, Hugh 149
Wolfe, Humbert 57
Wood, Susan 111, 152, 162
Wordsworth, William 47, 107

Young, Geoffrey Winthorpe 43